THE RESCUERS
THE WORLD'S TOP ANTI-TERRORIST UNITS

T0204561

LEROY THOMPSON

THE RESCUERS
THE WORLD'S TOP ANTI-TERRORIST UNITS

PALADIN PRESS
BOULDER, COLORADO

The Rescuers: The World's Top Anti-Terrorist Units
by Leroy Thompson
Copyright © 1986 by Leroy Thompson

ISBN 0-87364-394-1
Printed in the United States of America

Published by Paladin Press, a division of
Paladin Enterprises, Inc., P.O. Box 1307,
Boulder, Colorado 80306, USA.
(303) 443-7250

Direct inquiries and/or orders to the above address.

Photo credits:

Page 137: AP/Wide World Photo; pages 138–140: 22nd SAS;
Page 141: top, MOD; bottom, Australian SAS;
Page 142: Imperial War Museum; page 143: Carmelo Cerezo; page 144:
    AMI; page 145: AP/Wide World Photo; page 146: ECP; pages 147–148:
    U.S. Army;
Page 149: top, IDF; bottom, AP/Wide World Photo;
Page 150: 22nd SAS; page 152: top, AP/Wide World Photo; Page 203: AMI;
Page 205: top, Steyr; bottom, AMI;
Page 208: Beretta; page 213: Arcair Company; page 214: ECP;
Page 216: left column, center, Rene Smeets; top right, Adrian Bohlen.

Endsheet photo: Members of the Belgian ESI HRU, who use ballistic
vests, gas masks, Browning Hi-Powers, and Remington shotguns, are
shown preparing for an assault. Photo courtesy of AMI.

Contents

Introduction

As the threat of terrorism has grown, so has the interest in those elite military and police units formed to combat terrorism. Because of the secrecy which surrounds them, however, very little information has been available about most anti-terrorist units. There have been books written about Delta (United States), the SAS (Great Britain), GSG-9 (West Germany), and GIGN (France), and these have given the public a glimpse into the training and skills of a top-flight HRU (Hostage Rescue Unit). Occasionally, a rescue mission will make headlines (sometimes in regard to unsuccessful missions, such as in the disastrous Egyptian "rescue" attempt on Malta), but the information about the HRUs themselves is generally sketchy or distorted. For many, however, these glimpses have just whetted the appetite for information.

Even the designations for most countries' anti-terrorist units have remained unknown until now. This secrecy stems from obvious necessity as well as the less obvious awareness of the fickle nature of the public. Since surprise is an important weapon in the anti-terrorist arsenal, secrecy is important to protect the "tricks of the trade." In many countries, secrecy is also important to protect the families of HRU members from retaliation by terrorists. A more subtle need for secrecy also stems from the ambivalent view many citizens take of anti-terrorist units. Although these citizens may scream for protection from the terrorist threat, they are suspicious of elite police or military units which they perceive as possible tools for repression. Although this view is most common in the Third World, such fears have also been expressed in some of the Western European democracies.

In *The Rescuers: The World's Top Anti-Terrorist Units,* I have tried to give the reader the most comprehensive pictures possible of the training, equipment, and tactics of the world's hostage rescue units. In many cases, I have had to leave out information or gloss over certain tactics for security purposes. Even so, I think it is quite likely that this work will become standard reading throughout the HRU and intelligence community and, no doubt, the terrorist community as well. For this latter group, I would emphasize that no matter how much information I've included herein, all the good HRUs have a lot of technological and tactical tricks available which I haven't even hinted at. I hope, in fact, that by my offering some insight into HRU capabilities, government support for such units may be increased and some terrorists may consider other lines of work. I must emphasize here, too, that for a country to maintain a viable anti-terrorist capability, strong government support is a necessity since the unit must be allowed the funds and manpower to retain the peak efficiency necessary to carry out extremely difficult and complex operations. Budget cutting, unfortunately, usually means less training and, frequently, the splitting up of the HRU as a full-time unit. If a unit is split and only brought together periodically to train, the razor edge is dulled, as is its rescue capability.

I have, no doubt, stepped on some toes in my evaluations of units, though I have tried to be as objective as possible. For the sake of security and accuracy, my manuscript has been read by members of the HRUs and intelligence agencies of more than a dozen countries. I have, of necessity, not discussed many sensitive areas of HRU tactics and equipment, but, whenever possible, I have included all information not vital to operational security. Too often, information is classified which doesn't need to be. So many lives ride on an HRU's skill and on surprise when it goes in, however, that security is extremely important in this case. I realize many readers will crave even more information; to them I can only say that everything I felt could be included without compromising a unit's abilities to carry out its mission has been included. In a very few cases I have been asked to omit sensitive information, and I have complied, but, for the most part, I have received constructive suggestions which have helped the book immensely.

Since I am far more interested in showing the "nuts and bolts" of how an HRU operates, I have avoided what I would term the "think tank commandos" who theorize about anti-terrorism and compile studies on anti-terrorist strategy. Don't get me wrong; their studies are important, and I don't denigrate them. However, I'm interested here in the tactics of anti-terrorism and the hard men who implement these tactics. It is important that the HRU understand what the terrorist might do and how he might do it so that he can be countered. The HRU member, however, must retain his perspective about terrorists without too much concern about the sociological basis for the terrorist's beliefs. The bottom line for the HRU is that the terrorist is a target, and the primary value of the social sciences is to allow the anti-terrorist warrior to focus on the target better.

Because of the nature of their professions, I cannot thank those who have given assistance by name; it's far better that their identities remain hidden behind their balaclavas. (Should any terrorists foolishly commit acts against the countries these men serve, however, they may get to meet them, though the acquaintance may terminate rather abruptly.) For their help, I say, "Thanks," and for the job they're doing, I say, "Drive on!"

CHAPTER 1
The Threat

T he word *terrorist* is a loaded term since it is a label that often depends on the perspective of the "victim." American patriots—such as the Minute Men, for example—were terrorists by the English definition, and both the British SOE (Special Operations Executive) and American OSS (Office of Strategic Services) were formed during World War II to encourage acts of terrorism against the Japanese and Germans. The U.S. Army Special Forces has the primary mission of training indigenous elements to commit acts of terrorism against the occupying power. Ironically, many of the techniques used by modern terrorists originated during the Jewish struggle to end the British Mandate in Palestine. Israel now considers itself a bastion against terrorism, yet ask any member of the British 6th Airborne Division who served in Palestine to name some terrorists and familiar names such as Menachem Begin and Golda Meir will probably be muttered along with some invectives.

Early in this century, anarchists, communists, and fascists all used bombs and other terrorist tactics in an attempt to gain political power, while the IRA (Irish

Republican Army) has been using bombs and guns throughout most of this century. The IRA is, of course, the classic example of a group whose members are viewed as "terrorists" in one quarter and patriots in another.

The record for longevity among terrorist groups is not, however, held by the IRA. One of today's pre-eminent "bogeymen"—the Shi'ite Muslim groups, such as the "Islamic Jihad"—can trace their lineage all the way back to the Medieval Assassins cult which made organized terrorism and assassination both a religion and a big business.

Although this book is not the place to trace the various Communist "national liberation" movements and guerrilla movements of the 1940s, 50s, and 60s, they must be mentioned since many of the current urban terrorist movements can trace some lineage to such insurgencies as the Mau Mau, Huks, Viet Cong, Khmer Rouge, or FLN. There are ironies in the rise of terrorism, too. The World War II OSS and SOE were formed for the purpose of exporting terrorism in the form of guerrilla forces in occupied territories. In simple terms these clandestine services were in the business of terrorism against the Germans, Japanese, and Italians. Soviet Partisans and French Maquis, lauded as heroes in World War II, were forerunners of today's guerrilla warriors and, to some extent, of today's terrorists. Even more ironically, the U.S. Special Forces which were formed to raise and train guerrillas (terrorists by definition of the target governments) now find themselves in Operational Detachment Delta assigned to anti-terrorist duties. When captured during World War II, members of the SAS were shot as terrorists by the Germans; now the SAS is comprised of the world's foremost anti-terrorist warriors. Israel's anti-terrorist forces can trace their own lineage almost directly to clandestine units which carried out acts of terrorism against the British in Palestine.

For the purposes of this book, it isn't really necessary to spend too much time defining terrorism or analyzing its philosophical implications. This book is most concerned with military or police units whose job it is to rescue hostages. As a result, those who take hostages for political or criminal ends may become the enemy—the target if you will—for the HRU.

In many ways, however, terrorism as it is often thought of today arose in conjunction with the spread of international air travel. Terrorists could now easily seize an extremely expensive piece of hardware, along with hundreds of passengers—often nationals of a country the terrorist group harbors a grudge against—and take them to a country sympathetic or at least neutral toward its aim. While the world watches via satellite television links, the terrorists can present their demands and philosophy to the largest possible audience.

The modern era of aircraft hijacking for political purposes really began in 1958 when Fidel Castro subtly began to encourage hijackings to Cuba. Palestinian terrorists soon adopted the hijacking of airliners as a tactic, especially after the 1967 Six Day War and "Black September," the month in which King Hussein crushed militant Palestinians in Jordan. The Popular Front for the Liberation of Palestine (PFLP) carried out the first of the Islamic terrorist attacks on an airliner on 23 July 1968 when an El Al 707 was hijacked to Algiers. At first, the PFLP attacks were just against El Al airliners, but as Israel tightened security and put armed guards aboard El Al flights, the terrorists began to look for other "softer" targets. U.S., Swiss, and British airliners were soon hijacked, including a TWA 747 which was seized after taking off from Schipol Airport in Amsterdam, forced to land at Cairo, and then blown up.

The combination of hijackings and the internal security threat posed by the Palestinians caused King Hussein of Jordan to take Draconian measures in September 1970, when he took the reins off the Arab Legion and allowed it to clean the Palestinian guerrillas out of Jordan. As a retaliatory arm of Al Fatah, "Black September" was formed in response to Hussein's actions. Despite numerous assassination attempts, however, Hussein proved a tough opponent and the Arab Legion proved too tough so that most of Black September's acts were directed against Israel or the West.

"Black September" began the practice of hijacking an airliner and holding its passengers hostage to demand the release of fellow terrorists who had been imprisoned for prior terrorist acts, thereby beginning a vicious cycle of terrorism breeding terrorism. The fact that South Yemen, Iraq, Libya, and Algeria offered sympathetic havens for these hijacked airliners helped make such acts easier to commit.

"Black September" wrote its name in bold, blood-red letters into the annals of terrorism with the 1972 murder of 11 Israeli Olympic athletes at the Munich Olympic Games, an act which prompted both Israel and West Germany to drastically upgrade their ability to respond to terrorist attacks. (Incidentally, it was also this act which prompted this author, a former Olympic hopeful, to offer his special operations training on anti-terrorist projects.) That year had also brought to light a graphic illustration of the cooperation between terrorists when a Japanese Red Army suicide attack was launched at Israel's Lod Airport, resulting in the death or injury of about 100 people. This attack was carried out as a "favor" for the Popular Front for the Liberation of Palestine and marked the first time the world at large became aware of the underground terrorist cartel which cooperated to commit acts of terrorism.

To finance their terrorist organizations, many groups used bank robbery or kidnapping, especially the Latin American and Western European terrorist groups. Kidnappings such as that of Quebec's Minister of Labor Pierre Laponte by the Quebec liberation group known as FLQ or of Aldo Moro by the Red Brigades, of course, were motivated by political rather than monetary considerations. Groups such as the SLA (Symbionese Liberation Army) in the United States and M19 in

Colombia, however, used bank robberies and kidnappings to raise funds for "the cause." The PLO (Palestine Liberation Organization) and the IRA have normally used somewhat more sophisticated methods to raise funds, including "donations" solicited from affluent Palestinians or Irishmen overseas, though the IRA has carried out its share of bank robberies. The U.S. organization known as NORAID, for example, has long been a prime source of IRA funds.

The 1970s saw the culmination of the use of hostages by terrorist groups in an attempt to force governments to accede to their demands. In addition to the massacre of Israeli hostages at Munich, other large-scale hostage incidents of the 1970s were:

1. the taking of 11 OPEC ministers hostage in Vienna in December 1975 by terrorism's super star "Carlos";
2. the takeover of the Saudi Arabian embassy in Khartoum in March 1973, and the shooting of American and Belgian diplomats there;
3. the takeover of the French embassy in the Hague in September 1974 by Japanese Red Army terrorists;
4. the occupation of the West German embassy in Stockholm, and the murder of two diplomats by members of the Baader-Meinhof Gang in April 1975;
5. the seizure of a train by South Moluccans during December 1975 in Holland;
6. the hijacking of an Air France plane to Entebbe in June 1976;
7. another train seizure as well as a school seizure by South Moluccans in Holland during May 1977;
8. the hijacking of a Japan Air Lines plane by JRA (Japanese Red Army) terrorists in September 1977;
9. the hijacking of a Lufthansa plane by the PFLP as a "favor" to the Baader-Meinhof Gang in

October 1977; and

10. the occupation of the American embassy in Teheran by Revolutionary Guards in November 1979.

The above-mentioned hostage situations account for only a small percentage of the terrorist incidents involving hostages during that period. Of special interest for purposes of this book are those incidents at Mogadishu, Entebbe, Holland, and Iran, which resulted in the use of counter-terrorist units which had also arisen during the 1970s in an attempt by governments to counter the terrorist threat.

Outright murders, bombings, and kidnappings accounted for many other well-known incidents during this same period. Among the more noteworthy were the following:

1. the August 1973 attack on passengers debarking from a TWA flight from Tel Aviv in Athens;

2. the attempt in September 1973 by members of "Black September" in Rome to shoot down an El Al airliner with SAM-7s;

3. the firebombing of a Pan Am plane and the hijacking of a Lufthansa plane in December 1973 in Rome by members of the NAYLP (note Abu Nidal, who would later make headlines as the brains behind the *Achille Lauro* hijacking, played a key role in this operation);

4. the assassination of Spanish Prime Minister Luis Carrero Blanco by terrorists from the Basque ETA in December 1973;

5. the kidnapping in Berkeley, California, in February 1974 of Patty Hearst by the SLA;

6. the murder of 18 people and wounding of 16 others at a residential building in Israel during April 1974 by PFLP-GC (Popular Front for the Liberation of Palestine-General Command);

7. the blowing up of a TWA airliner with 88 aboard in October 1974 by NAYLP;

8. the murder of the Chief of the Argentine Fed-

eral Police in June 1976 by the ERP;

9. the kidnapping and murder of German business-
man Hans-Martin Schleyer in September/Octo-
ber 1977 by members of the Baader-Meinhof
Gang;

10. the murder of Judge Rosano Bernardi and the
kidnapping of Aldo Moro in March 1978 in
Rome by members of the Red Brigades;

11. the shooting down of a Rhodesian airliner in
January 1979 by ZANU (Zimbabwe African
National Union);

12. the murder of the British ambassador in The
Hague by Provos and Red Help in March 1979;

13. the bomb attack on General Alexander Haig's
auto in Belgium in June 1979 by Baader-Meinhof Gang members;

14. the murder of Earl Mountbatten in August 1979
by Provos; and

15. the occupation of the Great Mosque at Mecca
in December 1979.

Once again, these incidents were selected from
many hundreds which took place in the 1970s to illustrate the extent to which terrorism had become a threat
to world order. The last item mentioned is of special
interest since the occupation marked the arrival of
terrorism by radical Moslems at the very heart of Islam.

During the 1980s, the threat of terrorism has continued to hang over the Western democracies like a sword
of Damocles. More and more, too, Libya's Muammar
Qaddafi has become the puppet master for many of the
world's terrorist groups and a financial benefactor for
many others. The Ayatollah Khomeini, on the other
hand, might be termed the spiritual leader for Islamic
terrorists. Carrying out anti-terrorist missions may cut
off a tentacle, but to deal a severe blow to the terrorist
octopus as a whole the brain centers in Libya and Iran
must be struck. The key roles played by the "Colonel"
and the "Mad Mullah" in the spread of terrorism in
recent years are clearly apparent if one looks at most of

the incidents. In April 1980 for example, the Iranian embassy in London came under occupation by Iranian militants. Throughout this period, Libyan hit teams sent to eliminate opponents of Colonel Qaddafi continued to operate in Europe. Qaddafi would later precipitate another incident in London involving an embassy in April 1984 when Libyan "diplomats" (terms which are seemingly self-contradictory) fired from the Libyan embassy, killing a British policewoman. An upsurge in right-wing terrorism was also seen in 1980 when a bomb went off at the Bologna railway station in August and another in September in Munich. The year 1980 was one which made the United States constantly aware of terrorism as the American hostage situation in Iran dragged on and played a large part in costing President Carter reelection.

Although other Iranian- and Libyan-backed incidents kept the cancer of terrorism growing, the U.S. Army in Europe also had to face a renewed RAF (Red Army Faction) assault on U.S. military installations in Europe during 1981. U.S. military personnel were not spared either as Brigadier General Dozier was kidnapped by the Red Brigades in Italy, a country which also suffered the year's most newsmaking terrorist incident when an attempt was made on the Pope's life. Civil aviation continued to be a primary target of terrorists in 1981 as there were 32 aircraft hijackings, 33 explosions on aircraft or in airports or airline offices, and six terrorist attacks against airports. Still, due to stepped-up airport security, terrorist incidents involving aircraft had begun to decline during the 1980s.

Within the U.S. itself, the period between 1978 and 1982 saw 243 terrorist attacks take place, of which almost half were committed by Puerto Rican separatist groups such as the FALN.

During the early months of 1982, U.S. installations in Central America came under increasing terrorist pressure, including a small arms and RPG-2 attack on the U.S. embassy in Guatemala City on 31 March. In fact, the U.S. became a target for terrorists all over the world, though certainly not the only target. More and more, too, the Western Alliance realized links existed between the KGB and terrorism as the conspiracy to assassinate the Pope was revealed and terrorist attacks against NATO installations and personnel were stepped up. The years 1982 and 1983 marked the IRA's return to an intensive bombing campaign within England; bombs detonated against the Household Cavalry in Hyde Park in July 1982 and against Christmas shoppers at Herrods department store in December 1983 caused special outrage.

Terrorism in Lebanon, as a result of the conflict in that country (especially by Shi'ites loyal to the Ayatollah Khomeini), caused hundreds of U.S. deaths during the 1980s. It has finally made Americans realize what the taking of the American embassy in Iran should mean: that the United States is in an undeclared war against Iran, one that we're fighting with our hands tied because we abide by international law while our opponent does not. The murder of a U.S. assistant military attaché in Paris in January 1982 by a group calling itself the Lebanese Armed Revolutionary Faction, the bombing of the U.S. embassy in Beirut in April 1983, the bombing of the U.S. Marine barracks and French paratroop barracks in October 1983, and the hijacking of a Kuwaiti airliner in December 1984 (resulting in the deaths of two Americans) have brought home the point that retaliatory and pre-emptive actions are necessary. Arguing about the ethics of action against Iran and Libya is equivalent to arguing about the ethics of killing a pack of rabid dogs which threaten one's life, yet such arguments continue while more Americans are killed by terrorists.

The Armenian Secret Army has increasingly taken its historical vendetta against the Turks afield during the last few years, striking at consuls (even "honorary" ones) in many countries. The Armenians have also widened their campaign to include broader terrorist acts, such as the bomb planted at Paris's Orly Airport in July 1983. In addition to the renewed IRA bombings and the one at Orly, 1983 and 1984 also saw members of the South Korean cabinet killed by a bomb in October in Burma and FALN bombs at the U.S. Capitol and in New York City in November 1983.

Perhaps the two incidents which brought the threat of terrorism home to Americans most dramatically, however, were the hijacking of a TWA flight in June 1985 by Shi'ites and the hijacking of the cruise ship *Achille Lauro* in October 1985 by the PLO. Each of these incidents resulted in the death of an American citizen. In response to the *Achille Lauro* incident, the U.S. was galvanized into action with the forcing down of the Egyptian airliner carrying the hijackers. It is hoped that such acts will help mark a tougher U.S. line against terrorism, a line that includes action rather than talk. The fact that over 7,000 acts of terrorism have been committed during the last 20 years, only a small percentage of which have been enumerated here, certainly should highlight the need for well-trained anti-terrorist forces and leaders with the courage to use them.

Although the terrorist threat has burgeoned over the last 30 years, the rise of the national hostage rescue unit has only occurred during the last 15 years. The event which was probably the greatest early stimulus to the rise of the HRU was the massacre of Olympic athletes by Black September in Munich during 1972. Israel and West Germany especially took the lead in developing HRUs after Munich. Britain and France also saw the need early in the 1970s to form a credible anti-terrorist deterrent. Munich was one stimulus for the creation of HRUs, but so were embassy sieges in Paris and IRA problems in Britain. Throughout the 1970s, the rest of the Western democracies began to develop their own deterrent. The U.S. lagged behind many of the European democracies in forming an HRU since terrorism didn't seem to be a major threat to our country. It was not until 1977, in fact, that the U.S.

government suddenly realized the need for a major HRU.

As national prestige became more involved in the ability to rescue hostages, the Third World began to develop its own deterrent forces. The taking hostage of the OPEC ministers by Carlos and the occupation of the Great Mosque made pro-Western Middle Eastern rulers realize that their countries were not exempt from acts of terrorism; the formation of HRUs in many Middle Eastern countries followed soon thereafter.

Today, almost every country in the world has some unit in the national police or military designated to carry out hostage rescue. The quality of these units, of course, varies greatly, and in some cases hostages might literally be in more danger of being shot accidentally by the rescuers than intentionally by the hijackers.

A subtle new form of power-brokering has emerged, too, as a result of the new stress on HRUs. The most successful major HRUs have found themselves called upon to train Third World anti-terrorist units and thus be in a position to subtly spread their country's influence. Such training missions, of course, have all sorts of residual benefits in intelligence gathering, weapons sales, and networking which may be greatly out of proportion to the size of the training team.

As the fear of terrorism has grown, so has the psychological need (among the citizens of Western democracies especially; but also in the Third World) to believe that the government can control the forces of chaos manifested in the form of terrorism. The HRU has, in effect, become the government's champion in the war against terrorism. As a result, the future of a government may quite often rest on how well the government itself, or its HRU functioning as an extension of the government, handles a terrorist threat. Look, for example, at the fall of the Italian government as a result of its handling of the *Achille Lauro* hijacking. Closer to home, it is quite likely that had Delta's Iranian rescue mission been successful, Jimmy Carter would have been re-elected president. The HRU is important because it saves lives, but it is also important as a symbol of a country's will and the ability to implement that will.

The trend during the 1980s has been for the United States to be singled out as a target of terrorism. External threats from Iranian- and Libyan-backed terrorist groups are very real, and both Delta and the FBI HRT are kept at a state of constant readiness to deal with such threats. There are also many internal threats to the U.S. in addition to international terrorist groups: Ultra-right-wing groups (such as the Posse Commitatus and the Covenant-the-Sword-and-the-Arm-of-the-Lord) as well as militant black groups (such as "MOVE") are also threats since their members can move more freely in this country than can foreign terrorists. In many cases, their confrontations come with police SWAT teams rather than national HRUs, but the step from barricading themselves in a rural or urban commune and firing on the police and taking hostages or hijacking an airliner is not that long a one.

The number of Cuban criminals and/or agents allowed into this country during the Carter administration offers another threat which may have to be dealt with by HRUs; the new rash of aircraft hijackings to Cuba offers ample proof of this danger.

The United States, Western Europe, and the West's allies in the Far East and Middle East are all vulnerable to acts of terrorism.

Oil facilities, for example, offer a juicy target for terrorists. Offshore rigs in the North Sea and Gulf of Mexico, refineries, super tankers, oil fields; all offer prime terrorist targets. Power facilities, especially nuclear ones, are another likely terrorist target.

The fact that many terrorists are disillusioned former students, many of whom are quite intelligent, offers the possibility that a terrorist might have the knowledge or have received the training in Libya, Iran, or Moscow to cause a catastrophic incident by sabotaging a nuclear power plant. In 1980, the FBI actually thwarted a plan which involved the takeover of the nuclear submarine *USS Trepang,* firing a nuclear missile at a U.S. city, and selling the nuclear submarine to a foreign power. The possibility that terrorists can build a nuclear device also has to be considered since nuclear technology is more widely disseminated throughout the Third World. Generally, for the time being, however, it is assumed that only government-backed terrorists (i.e., Iran, Libya, and others) would be likely to obtain the necessary materials. It is more likely, however, that a nuclear weapon could be stolen or hijacked, a possibility which has formed the basis for a great many thrillers.

Another possible source of terrorist danger rests with chemical or biological weapons should they fall into the wrong hands. Threats and even attempts to introduce biological elements into water supplies have already taken place and are likely to again. Frighteningly, too, for someone with sufficient training in the biological sciences, dangerous biological agents can be developed relatively easily. Toxic chemical agents cause enough problems with regard to improper disposal of chemical wastes; yet in the hands of terrorists, such agents designed as weapons present an even more frightening scenario. (Some nerve gases, for example, can be produced relatively easily.)

The reliance placed on computer systems in the United States, Western Europe, and Japan also makes important central computers attractive targets to terrorists wishing to disrupt commerce or government operations. Multi-national U.S. businesses as symbols of capitalism are also attractive targets for terrorists, as are the executives of such companies.

U.S. embassies or the embassies of any country targeted by a terrorist group are appealing to terrorists in many ways. In such countries as Iran, of course, terrorists can count on active support from the government, while in many other countries terrorists attacking an embassy have received tacit governmental support. In other cases, the attack on an embassy has served the dual purpose of embarrassing the host government and harming the property and/or nationals of the country whose embassy was attacked.

Terrorists function best in free societies, yet their actions do much to destroy this freedom since often harsh measures are taken by democracies in an attempt to stamp out terrorism. The best alternative is an intelligence system which can keep track of terrorists and predict terrorist attacks far enough in advance, backed up by an unobtrusive, highly trained anti-terrorist unit which can carry out a surgical operation to free hostages or prevent terrorists from committing other acts against the state the anti-terrorist unit protects. America and her allies love liberty, and the protection of that liberty—both physical and psychological—rests very heavily on the shoulders of Delta, FBI HRT (Hostage Response Team), SAS, GSG-9, GIGN, GEO, ESI, and other such units discussed here in *The Rescuers*.

CHAPTER 2

Five Classic Rescues

I n the nearly one-and-one-half decades that have passed since the Munich massacre, the Western democracies and most of their Third World allies have worked very hard to develop a credible anti-terrorist capability. Despite the untold hours spent in training and the untold millions of dollars spent on equipment and salaries, the number of major successful operations carried out by such units is only about a dozen. The limited number of successes does not in any way, however, indicate that highly trained HRUs are not useful. Much of the value of such units is in deterrence, and there is no objective way to evaluate how many hostage incidents have been avoided because of the existence of a unit. The value of units as deterrents when used on VIP protection or installation security assignments must also be borne in mind.

Unfortunately, however, many governments, especially in the Third World, find it difficult to justify the expense of keeping such a unit of highly trained police or soldiers (particularly when in many Third World countries most police or military are not too capable) together and sharp for that terrorist incident which may not come for years or may not come at all. As a result, HRUs which were highly competent when formed and trained often get dispersed to perform various security functions and only come together occasionally, if at all, to train.

It is therefore the few major rescues which have taken place which justify the existence of expensive HRUs to the politicians and the public and which send an emphatic message to terrorists. It is unfortunate, too, that the failures always receive far more notoriety than the successes. The Egyptian rescue attempts on Cyprus and Malta, for example, both proved debacles of major proportions, while the failure of the U.S. rescue attempt into Iran dealt a severe blow to this country's anti-terrorist credibility.

Of the successful rescues which have been carried out, five in particular have become classic examples of anti-terrorist tactics and planning. As a result of these successes, it should be noted, the HRUs of the five countries carrying out the operations—France, Israel, Holland, Germany, and Great Britain—have received acceptance as the world's foremost experts on anti-terrorism. Because of their importance in the development of anti-terrorist training and tactics, each of these five operations will be discussed and analyzed below. One of the most important points to note in reading about these five "classic" rescues is that despite intensive planning and rehearsals, flexibility was required in each operation to allow for unexpected problems.

DJIBOUTI

On the morning of 3 February 1976, a school bus carrying thirty school children (the sons and daughters of French Air Force personnel) was hijacked in Djibouti by four F.L.C.S. (Front for the Liberation of the Coast of Somalia) terrorists. Unless their demands (which included the release of "political prisoners") were met, they threatened to slit the children's throats. The terrorists stopped the bus within sight of the Somali border and were joined by two other terrorists who crossed from Somalia.

In response to the hijacking, local French Foreign Legion units were alerted, and Lt. Prouteau of GIGN (Groupement D'Intervention De La Ger.darmerie Nationale) and nine of his men were flown to Djibouti. As soon as possible, Prouteau carried out a reconnaissance of the area surrounding the bus. The terrain presented many problems, both for positioning snipers and for carrying out a clandestine approach prior to an assault since it was very flat with virtually no cover. There were some fairly large rocks and an embankment about 200 meters from the bus which would offer some cover. Prouteau's plan, which evolved after his recce of the site, was to place his nine men in cover behind the rocks and embankment and to attempt to take out all of the terrorists simultaneously at long range.

GIGN has a fairly set tactical doctrine in such situations, and Prouteau brought it into play at Djibouti. Each sniper was assigned a certain area of the bus to cover. Each terrorist was also assigned a number. Using laryngophones which left their hands free to work their FR-F1 rifles, the GIGN marksmen would then say the number of the target in their crosshairs into the microphone. Prouteau would only give the order to fire when all targets were covered simultaneously. However, there proved to be a certain amount of difficulty keeping track of the terrorists since at least four remained on the bus at all times while the others might go to the Somali border post nearby for a break. The Somalis were obviously aiding the terrorists, but members of the 2nd REP (2nd Foreign Legion Paratroop Regiment) were on the scene to deal with them if necessary.

Throughout the day, the GIGN snipers waited in the heat for the instant when the simultaneous shot would present itself. The comings and goings of the terrorists and the silhouettes of the children combined to make the simultaneous kill needed for success virtually impossible. Finally, at 1400 the terrorists agreed to allow a meal in for the children. Tranquilizers were put in the food in hopes that the children would fall asleep, thus removing their silhouettes from the bus windows. After a ten-hour wait, the long-awaited simultaneous shot presented itself at 1547, and Prouteau gave the order to fire. Four terrorists aboard the bus were killed instantly with head shots. A fifth terrorist who was just outside the bus was also quickly eliminated.

The Somali border guard post instantly took the GIGN men under fire, pinning them down before they could get to the bus. GIGN snipers, however, returned the fire, cutting down ten Somalis, while members of the 2nd REP took other Somalis under fire. Realizing the need to rescue the children, Prouteau and two of his men rushed across the 200 meters to the bus which the sixth terrorist had reboarded under the cover of the Somali fire. Prouteau and his men quickly cut the terrorist down, but not before one little girl was killed. Had the Somalis not intervened, GIGN would have carried off the rescue with no loss of life, but Prouteau's quick actions still allowed them to save 29 small hostages.

Analysis

Because of the publicity surrounding the Entebbe raid, GIGN's rescue in Djibouti is frequently forgotten, and Israel is given credit for the first successful anti-terrorist operation in another country. The Djibouti operation remains a classic, however, since Prouteau made excellent use of GIGN's skill at long-range marksmanship to exercise the only option available in the flat terrain in which the bus was parked. The fact that GIGN members are also trained for the assault and in quick-reaction shooting enabled them to react quickly to rush the bus and neutralize the remaining terrorist when he was unexpectedly encountered. Also, the fact that the GIGN men managed to account for ten Somalis with precision shooting, despite being under heavy fire, is a comment on their coolness under pressure. GIGN's versatility is apparent in the fact that ten men were considered a sufficient number to carry out the rescue— once again, an argument in favor of GIGN's policy of training every man for every job.

The massive retaliation on the Somali border post by the 2nd REP and GIGN, which accounted for a possible East German or Soviet "advisor" to the terrorists as well as numerous Somali troops, was an excellent object lesson to states which choose to support terrorism.

ENTEBBE

Though not the first major successful anti-terrorist strike, the Israeli raid at Entebbe Airport in Uganda to free 103 hostages on 4 July 1976 is of extreme significance for the purposes of this book because of the magnitude of the operation. The Air France plane involved had been hijacked on 27 June 1976 with 254 passengers and crew aboard and forced to land at Entebbe Airport with the compliance of the Ugandan government and its ruler Idi Amin. The hijackers were a combination of PLO and Baader-Meinhof terrorists who were attempting to gain the freedom of 53 Palestinians or other terrorists from prisons in Israel and elsewhere.

Israel was diametrically opposed to dealing with terrorists, so a military option was considered from the beginning, though the large number of hostages would make such a strike very difficult. Still, Israeli intelligence began to assemble info on Entebbe, the hostages, hijackers, and Ugandan troops near the airfield. A special strike force also was assembled and began training in the desert for a possible rescue operation. In the meantime, however, Israel agreed to negotiate to buy time.

One break for the Israelis was that the Entebbe Airport had been built by an Israeli construction firm, so some intelligence on the airport was readily available. U.S. sources also made information available, including satellite photos of Entebbe. Planning for a possible strike became easier on 30 June when non-Jewish hostages—except for the Air France crew which refused to leave unless all were freed—were released. Not only did the reduced numbers make a rescue more feasible, but anti-terrorism specialist Maj. Gen. Rehavam Zeevi gained valuable intelligence about the terrorists, Ugandan soldiers, and the airport lounge where the hostages were being held by interviewing the freed hostages.

In the meantime, the strike force for "Operation Thunderbolt" was undergoing intensive training in the desert. Drawn from the 35th Parachute Brigade and the Golani Infantry Brigade, the one-hundred-plus men of the strike force worked on speedily clearing the C-130s which would carry them into action, assaulting and securing the terminal building, and moving the hostages out safely—all in under 55 minutes, since any delay could increase the risks of reinforcements from the Ugandan Army arriving and overwhelming the strike force.

The Air Force crew which would fly the strike force to Entebbe also practiced navigating without aid of air-traffic controllers since they would have to fly clandestinely. Because fuel would prove to be a problem, members of the strike force learned how to operate refuelling equipment of the type to be found at Entebbe.

Using a scale model of the terminal and airport, the plan evolved using three C-130s to carry the strike elements and to evacuate the hostages, while a command and control 707 would circle overhead. The timetable which developed during training called for the strike force to:

- secure the terminal building within ten minutes of landing
- evacuate the hostages within another 20 minutes
- check the terminal building for stragglers and mop up within ten minutes

- load the strike force back on the aircraft and take off within 12 more minutes.

Primary weapons selected for the raid were reportedly MAC-10, rather than Uzi SMGs, and Galil assault rifles, the latter equipped with night sights. By the time the strike force carried out a full dress rehearsal, it had the time down under 55 minutes, so it was ready to go. Realizing it needed an edge to quickly gain access to the terminal, the strike force had also acquired a black Mercedes which had been painted and trimmed to look exactly like one used by Idi Amin. The part it would play would prove to be critical.

Early in July, Israeli agents—presumably Mossad but possibly from the GHQ Recon/Unit 269 anti-terrorist force—infiltrated Entebbe Airport and gained close-range intelligence. These agents—and others—remained in position so that they could mine approach roads and cut telephone lines into Entebbe shortly before "Thunderbolt" struck. On 3 July, the final decision was made to carry out the raid, though the actual operation was already in motion at the time. The three C-130s and the 707 took off at 3:00 P.M. on 3 July. Another 707 equipped as a hospital plane also took off for Nairobi so it would be nearby to handle the large number of casualties anticipated. Agents including GHQ/269 Recon special strike units disguised as El Al crewmen infiltrated Nairobi Airport as well. Should it be necessary to refuel at Nairobi and should Kenya not grant permission to do so, these men were prepared to seize the airport.

The C-130s swooped in over Lake Victoria, confusing the Entebbe tower personnel by claiming to be a flight carrying released Palestinians. Just after midnight on 4 July, two C-130s landed on the main runway, while a third landed on a disused runway. After taxiing as close to the terminal as possible, one C-130 dropped its ramp and disgorged the black Mercedes which appeared to be Amin's personal limo. Instead, it was a Trojan Horse containing Israeli commandos. As the Ugandan guards came to attention for the limo, they were hosed down with automatic weapons fire from Israeli strike elements dressed as PLO men and riding in escorting Land Rovers.

Using the surprise gained by this ploy, commandos burst into the terminal, taking out the terrorists with a hail of fire. The commandos kept shouting, "We're Israelis!" and ordering the hostages to keep down, but three of the hostages stood up and were killed. As the assault force struck, another strike unit hit the tower and secured it to prevent controllers from radioing for help. Other commandos set up a roadblock between a nearby Ugandan Army barracks and the airport.

The hostages were hustled aboard the C-130s while sporadic firing continued and another Israeli strike team blew up 11 MIGs at the airport to forestall pursuit. By the time the shooting had stopped, 20 Ugandan soldiers had been killed, along with the terrorist guards, and more than 100 Ugandans had been wounded. The only Israeli killed in action was the strike force commander, LTC Yehonatan Netanyahu, though some others were wounded.

Timing on the raid was perfect; the C-130 carrying the hostages cleared the runway at Entebbe 53 minutes after landing. The strike force members took a little longer as they secured the area, mopped up, and fingerprinted the dead terrorists before rolling up their perimeter. As the strike force's C-130s took off, the final one had a few tense moments as the runway lights were cut during takeoff and the pilot had to rely on instinct to follow the runway.

Fortunately, Kenya allowed the planes to refuel before they proceeded on to Israel, where the hostages and rescuers were met with great jubilation.

Analysis

The Entebbe Raid was a watershed since it marked the first long-distance anti-terrorist strike to rescue hostages and gave hope that other such operations would prove feasible. In evaluating the Entebbe operation, however, it is necessary to bear certain factors in mind. First, the Israelis had excellent intelligence on the layout of the airport complex at Entebbe. Second, the lack of sophistication of the radar net over that part of Africa allowed the strike force to approach and land virtually undetected. The fact that Kenya—Uganda's neighbor—was not friendly to Amin's regime and thus would not tip off the Ugandans to anything seen on Kenyan radar screens was another key element. The ignorance of the Ugandan soldiers and fear of Idi Amin allowed the ruse with the limo to be successful, whereas in other circumstances it probably would not have been so. The isolation of Entebbe Airport also proved an aid to the operation since it proved relatively easy to cut off from rapid reinforcement.

Most critical, however, was the fact that no one expected the Israelis to mount a rescue. By being the first rescue mission of its type (unless one considers the Son Tay Raid, which Israel reportedly used as a model), the Entebbe Raid caught the terrorists and Ugandans completely off guard. After Entebbe, terrorists had to at least consider the possibility that a rescue mission would be carried out.

In no way, however, should these breaks detract from the excellent intelligence gathering and planning carried out by the Israelis nor from the professionalism displayed by the assault troops in their execution of the raid itself. They performed with precision and alacrity under very trying circumstances. The Israelis got a lot of breaks at Entebbe, but they also made a lot of their own luck, too. It took courage and determination to launch a raid over such a great distance and against such odds. As the United States found when it launched its abortive Iranian rescue mission, long-distance missions into a hostile country complicate a rescue geometrically since not only does the strike force have to carry out its mission effectively, but it has to be delivered to and extracted from the scene of the rescue. Of the five classic rescues to be discussed in this chapter, only Entebbe was carried out into a hostile environment. The other four were all within the country of the HRU or were within a friendly country which cooperated in allowing the rescue to take place.

DEPUNT TRAIN AND
BOVENSMILDE SCHOOL

On 23 March 1977, a Dutch train was hijacked between Groningen and Assen by nine South Moluccan terrorists, while an elementary school at Bovensmilde nearby was occupied simultaneously. Fifty-one hostages were taken on Train 747 and 110 at the school, though 106 of the school hostages were released unharmed a few days later when most of the children contracted a stomach virus.

The Dutch were very reluctant to use force to resolve these hostage crises, but as the negotiations dragged on for nearly three weeks, it became apparent that the situation on the train could degenerate into a massacre. Throughout the seige, the Royal Dutch Marines Close Combat Unit had been rehearsing assaults on an exact duplicate of the train at Gilze Rijin AFB nearby. Eight combat swimmers had approached the train via a canal which ran within 15 yards of the tracks and had placed sensitive listening devices. Special radar which would detect heat differentials in metal surfaces had been emplaced near the train as well so the terrorists' locations could be determined by the presence of their weapons. Other sophisticated detection devices were in use so that the Marines would know where the terrorists and hostages were likely to be should the Marines have to assault. When Dr. Dik Mulder, the psychiatrist who had been negotiating with the terrorists, decided the situation was such that the hostages were in danger, the Marines were finally given the "go" order to assault the train. Using night-vision goggles, the Marine five-man assault teams, totaling 40 to 50 men, approached the train during the night.

Once they were ready, six F104 Starfighters flew low over the train, kicking in their afterburners to keep the hostages' heads down and to distract the terrorists. The SAS had offered the assault team stun grenades, but the Dutch chose to use the jets instead.

As the jets roared overhead, police and Marine sharpshooters opened up on the areas of the train where the terrorists normally slept. At 4:53 A.M., the assault force blew the doors off the train with frame charges and went in with their Uzis blazing. On bullhorns, the Marines told the hostages to keep their heads down. Two hostages, however, panicked and were killed as they stood up. Interestingly, they were the two hostages psychological profiles had predicted would panic. Six of the terrorists were killed during the assault. Three surrendered, one after shooting a hostage, though not fatally.

Virtually simultaneously with the assault on the train, other Marines launched an assault in APCs on the school at Bovensmilde. Crashing through the wall with an APC, the Marines took the terrorists by surprise; three, in fact, were sleeping in their underwear. All four terrorists at the school were taken alive, and the four hostages were rescued unharmed.

Analysis

In breaking this dual siege, the Dutch Marines had to consider the possibility that if either the school or the train were taken down individually, the terrorists occupying the other might hear of the assault and execute the hostages. The length of the train made the planning of the assault somewhat more difficult, though the judicious use of technological aids enabled the Marines to do an effective job of identifying the locations of hostages and terrorists. The use of the F104s as a diversion proved relatively sound, too, since the natural reaction to the noise and vibration was to duck, thus forcing the hostages to get their heads down as the sharpshooters poured in fire. Stun grenades might not have been as effective since the compartmentalization of the train would have dissipated their effect. The F104s were also effective in that they allowed the fire to be poured into the terrorists' compartments prior to the actual assault, while the stun grenades would have been heaved in as the Marines went in.

From the point of view of showing national will, this assault was an especially important one, since the belief among the South Moluccans was that no matter how hard the Dutch government was pushed the force option would not be resorted to. Since the problem of Moluccan terrorism was one that had plagued Dutch society throughout the Seventies, the "get-tough" attitude illustrated by this assault was probably a necessity in order to send the South Moluccans a clear message.

MOGADISHU

On 13 October 1977, a Lufthansa 737 with 91 persons aboard was hijacked by four terrorists—two men and two women. After landing at various points in the Middle East, the terrorists finally forced the pilot to land the plane at Mogadishu Airport in Somalia. The pilot, Jurgen Schumann, was later executed by the terrorists as a direct result of the lack of restraint by the press, which had revealed that the pilot had managed to convey information about the terrorists via the radio.

By 1730 on 17 October, 29 members of GSG-9 plus 30 medical personnel had been flown to Mogadishu on a special Lufthansa 707. Fortunately, the Somalis were much more cooperative with the Germans than they had been with the French during the Djibouti school-bus hijacking. Somali commandos had, in fact, set up perimeter security around the entire area. As soon as the GSG-9 plane (which had been following the hijacked plane around the Middle East) landed, the German anti-terrorist force prepared for an immediate assault should the situation deteriorate aboard the plane. This, by the way, is SOP (standard operating procedure). Normally, an anti-terrorist unit will prepare an emergency assault plan ASAP and then will work on a more refined plan as time allows.

GSG-9 reconnaissance and sniper teams were quickly ordered into position as close to the plane as possible, while assault SETs prepared to go in. By 2205 the snipers and recon teams were in position, and by 2315 the assault SETs had begun their clandestine approach.

To stall for time, the terrorists had been led to believe that the fellow terrorists the hijackers were trying to free were being flown to Somalia. To further divert the terrorists, Somali troops at 2350 lit a fire about 100 meters in front of the hijacked aircraft. It was hoped that the terrorists would congregate in the cockpit to observe the fire and try to figure out what the Somalis were up to. The ruse worked perfectly, and the terrorists went to the cockpit.

Taking advantage of the distraction created by the fire, the assault teams silently approached the 737 from the rear and moved into position beneath the wings. Two SAS men—Maj. Alistair Morrison and Sgt. Barry Davies—were with the assault teams; when the "Go!" order was given from Ulrich Wegener, they launched stun grenades toward the cockpit window. Simultaneously, GSG-9 men placed rubber-coated-alloy assault ladders against the aircraft and forced entry through the emergency exit doors. A female terrorist was encountered almost immediately and eliminated, but the second female terrorist took cover in a toilet and opened fire, slightly wounding one GSG-9 trooper. Return fire seriously wounded her, however, and put her out of the fight.

In the cockpit, the terrorist leader—"Captain Mahmud"—sustained multiple hits from .38 Special rounds fired by the GSG-9 point man from his S&W Model 36. The loads, which were not Glasers or some other round offering good stopping power, did not instantly immobilize him, and he had a chance to throw two grenades. Fortunately, the two grenades rolled under seats where their force was cushioned. Realizing the lack of effect of his revolver, the point man had quickly taken the MP5 from his backup man and finished off "Captain Mahmud." The remaining terrorist had been personally eliminated by Col. Wegener with a head shot from his S&W Chief's Special.

Even before all of the terrorists had been eliminated, GSG-9 began hustling the hostages from the rear of the plane. Once it was secured, the plane was checked for explosives. Three hostages had been wounded during the assault but none had been killed. At 0012, the message "Springtime" had gone out, signaling that the assault had been a success. By 0313, the GSG-9 force had been loaded back onto its plane and took off to return to Bonn.

Analysis

It should be emphasized that the Mogadishu operation was successful because the Somali authorities cooperated with the West Germans and allowed GSG-9 to move into position and assault. The Somalis also actively cooperated in setting up perimeter security and in setting the fire which acted as a distraction for the terrorists. The excellent training of GSG-9 was, of course, critical in that the assault teams managed to carry out a very difficult approach silently, followed by a rapid breeching and securing of the aircraft. The only real problem encountered in the assault was the lack of stopping power displayed by the S&W .38 Special carried by some of the assault force. The quick reactions of the GSG-9 point man, however, allowed him to rectify this shortcoming with an MP5.

Of special importance is the fact that GSG-9 had trained intensively on different types of aircraft, including the 737, and was aware of the blind spots for approach, the points likely to cause vibration or noise, and the best methods for gaining entry. GSG-9's technological backup in the form of special ladders and stun grenades also proved invaluable.

Another subtle consideration in evaluating the Mogadishu rescue is that GSG-9 set a new standard for rescue ops in that no hostages were killed during the assault, while at Djibouti, Entebbe, and Train 747 at least one hostage had been killed during the assault. The murder of the Lufthansa pilot for trying to feed information useful to rescuers is also a point to be remembered since it illustrates the great harm which irresponsibility on the part of the press can do during a hostage situation.

PRINCES GATE

As has already been mentioned, members of the SAS had been present when the Royal Dutch Marines broke the siege on Train 747 and when GSG-9 went in at Mogadishu. The SAS's classic rescue, however, took place at home in London in front of millions who watched the operation on television. Considering the SAS desire for obscurity, the television coverage proved to be somewhat ironical.

The hostage situation had begun on 30 April 1980 when Iranians opposed to the regime of the Ayatollah Khomeini (and who according to some sources were working for Iraqi intelligence) had taken over the Iranian embassy in London, gaining 26 hostages in the process, including a British policeman and a British newscameraman. Due to medical problems, five of the hostages would be released relatively early in the siege.

The police constable on duty at the embassy had managed to radio an alert before he was taken by the terrorists, so the Metropolitan Police's D11 unit had taken up positions around the embassy fairly quickly. C13, the anti-terrorist squad of the Met, and C7, the Technical Support Branch, had also arrived to set up surveillance and CPs. The SAS received notice of the possible need for their services via the SAS old-boy network when a former SAS NCO, now a dog handler with the Met, telephoned the officers' mess at Hereford and tipped them to a situation which might demand their involvement.

The terrorists' demands included the freedom of 91 prisoners in Iran, something the British authorities had no control over. If these demands were not met, the terrorists were threatening to execute the hostages and blow up the embassy. The ex-SAS man who had first called his comrades proved correct in his surmise that the SAS would be called in. The on-alert SAS CRW Team— "Pagoda Troop"—was deployed to London and put on standby at a barracks in Regents Park. The anti-terrorist specialists carried out recces of the embassy and its surroundings in civilian clothes and constructed a scale model of the embassy at their temporary quarters. A London barracks was also turned into the "embassy" for practice assaults and clearance drills. As possible assault tactics evolved through discussion, frame charges of the proper sizes and blasting power for the embassy windows were prepared in case they might be needed to blow the windows during an assault. The layout of the embassy was studied intensively as well since its size—50 rooms—made an assault difficult to plan. Intelligence gained from microphones (some suspended down the chimneys) and other surveillance devices was fed to the assault team constantly to aid in planning possible assaults. Most of the intelligence-gathering hardware had been emplaced by C7, though the SAS had such equipment available should it be needed.

As the negotiations dragged on, the terrorists dropped their demand that the prisoners be freed in Iran, but they still wanted a mediator from a friendly Arab country. Since both the terrorists and potential mediators wanted safe conduct for the terrorists, this stipulation also met a dead-end. By 5 May—the sixth day of the siege—the terrorists were becoming frustrated and the situation in the embassy began to deteriorate. The terrorists renewed their threat to start executing the hostages, and at 1331 three shots were heard. The decision to send in the SAS, however, was not precipitated until 1850 when three more shots were heard, followed shortly by the body of the embassy press officer being thrown out the door. It later turned out that he had been killed by the earlier shots. Police negotiators immediately began stalling for time to prevent more killings. The negotiators told the terrorists that their demands were about to be met and that they needed to discuss details about arranging a plane to fly them out of the country. In actuality, the negotiators were stalling to allow the SAS assault teams to finalize preparations for going in.

Assault teams in position, "Operation Nimrod" began at 1923 as eight SAS men abseiled from the embassy roof to the first-floor balcony and ground floor terrace at the rear of the embassy. The teams operated in two-man units and prepared their frame charges to blow the windows. One member of this group, however, got tangled in the rope (reportedly because additional rope not up to normal SAS standards had been hurriedly purchased in London) and was dangling too near the windows, thus preventing the use of the frame charges to breach the windows. Quickly adjusting, the assault teams hacked and hammered their way in through the hardened windows, pitching in stun grenades and following them in with MP5s at the ready. The first two-man team found itself in a room they had thought contained hostages but, in actuality, did not. Even worse, egress from this room was blocked, thus slowing the assault momentarily. As soon as possible, this assault force headed for the telex room, which was known to hold the majority of the hostages. The leader of the terrorists was on a first-floor landing and spotted a member of the assault force coming through the window. As the terrorist prepared to fire at the SAS man, though, Police Constable Trevor Lock, who had been brought along to talk on the phone to the negotiators, tackled him, giving the SAS man time to fire a quick burst into the terrorist after calling to Lock to roll clear.

Meanwhile, four other SAS men had blown the windows on the first floor (U.S. second floor) of the embassy with frame charges. They had climbed onto the balcony from adjoining buildings. As soon as the windows had been blown, the assault team threw in stun grenades and then followed them in. A third assault party, meanwhile, crashed through the plaster and entered the embassy. Amidst the flash, bang of stun grenades, and haze of CS gas, the two-man assault teams systematically cleared the embassy room by room, dropping any terrorists encountered with bursts from their MP5s. The prime objective, however, remained the telex room where three terrorists held 15 male hostages. Realizing that an assault was in progress, the terrorists executed one hostage and wounded two others before the SAS broke into the telex room and eliminated two of the terrorists instantly. The third survived by mingling with the hostages. Two other terrorists had been eliminated during the room-clearing ops—one on the ground floor and another in an office at the back of the embassy.

Since they could not be sure the embassy was not wired with explosives or booby traps and they knew there was still one terrorist to be sorted from the hostages, the SAS quickly hustled the hostages out of the embassy by throwing them from assault trooper to assault trooper. Once the hostages were outside, they could be sorted out. This technique allowed the embassy to be cleared quickly (especially since a fire was now raging as a result of the use of the breaching charges and/or stun grenades) yet did not compromise security of the assault teams or police outside. Another consideration which had to be allowed for after the six-day siege was the possibility that the "Stockholm Syndrome" might have come into play, causing an affinity to develop between the hostages and the terrorists, whereby one or more hostages may cooperate with the terrorists. The possibility of a confederate within the embassy staff also had to be considered.

The embassy cleared, the SAS (after possibly a quick look for codebooks or other items of interest) cleared the embassy themselves. The whole assault took only 11 minutes. Delays gaining entry at the rear of the embassy may have cost one hostage his life, but the others were saved and the terrorists had been neutralized.

Analysis

Certain members of the press and even some of the hostages cried about the SAS's ruthlessness in killing five of the six terrorists. Such unrealistic views do not, of course, take into consideration the fact that the SAS had to quickly identify friend from foe in a fluid situation amidst flame and smoke in which terrorists might have had the means to detonate explosives or grenades even after throwing their weapons down. Once the terrorists started killing the hostages, they were justifiably "bought and paid for," and anyone not willing to admit that is very naive about terrorists and murderers of any ilk.

The SAS had previously lost men in similar assaults and their thoroughness is to be lauded. They had not been sent in to arrest anyone, just to get the hostages out alive. Normally, dead terrorists are better than live terrorists since they are no longer available to cause other terrorist acts in an attempt to free them from prison. The draconian fate dealt to the terrorists also signaled to any others contemplating such acts in Great Britain that a liberal and free society is not necessarily a weak society, a distinction most terrorists have trouble making without bloody object lessons. The only fault to be found in the killing of the five terrorists is that through the misguided loyalty of some hostages who shielded the sixth terrorist, he remained alive.

The SAS's intensive training in room-clearing tactics at their "Killing House" obviously paid dividends in the efficient way the embassy was cleared. Although intelligence provided by the high-tech hardware fell down on one or two points, it did allow the strike teams to head for the telex room where the majority of the hostages were held as soon as possible. The SAS's well-sharpened ability to act quickly and effectively under stress not only aided them during the room-clearing, but also when conditions prevented the use of the frame charges in the rear of the embassy.

If, as the author has been told, the rope which became entangled during the abseil from the roof was one acquired locally because more length was needed, the necessity for rigorous testing of HRU equipment is once again obvious since its failure during an assault can cost the lives of HRU members and hostages. It should be noted that to prevent such a recurrence, the SAS has been using a new braided line made by Marlow Rope Company. The SAS, of course, through its ops-research unit, tests equipment extensively and can thus normally be confident of the equipment that is issued. Still, the lesson to be learned is probably to assume that a situation well out of the ordinary may arise and equipment used to cope with it should be maintained.

The SAS doesn't court publicity, and the fact that the assault was televised certainly wasn't to be asked for. It did, however, have the dual purpose of reinforcing the message to other potential terrorists and giving the British public a shot of national pride in the SAS. All in all, that's not a bad dividend, especially since the SAS's attire did not allow any members of the unit to be compromised. Princes Gate was a well-planned operation, which was much more difficult than it might have appeared due to the size of the embassy. The SAS's intensive training paid off, but no matter how easy they made it look, it certainly wasn't so. It took countless hours in the Killing House and on practice assaults to have the skills used in those 11 minutes. That's the problem, in fact, of any HRU; years of training may have to be expended to be ready for a few minutes. *Who dares, wins,* is true; but so is *who sweats, wins* and certainly *who plans, wins.* The daring must be accomplished by capability; the SAS has both.

CONCLUSIONS

Other important rescues have taken place which might have been discussed in this chapter. The Israeli GHQ/269 Unit carried out an important rescue aboard a Sabena airliner at Lod Airport in 1972, for example. The Indonesians have carried out a successful operation aboard a hijacked airliner, as have the Venezuelans and a few others. The General Dozier rescue in Italy was an extremely important one since it marked the turning point in the battle against the Red Brigades. A very little-known, but important, rescue was that of some missionaries which was carried out by the Sudanese in 1983. It was very well executed, and it illustrated that Third World HRUs are capable of carrying out difficult operations effectively if their level of training is high enough.

The five operations discussed above have illustrated the importance of training, planning, proper equipment, and audacity on the part of the HRU. The importance of the location where the hostages are being held should also have become apparent since the best HRU in the world cannot succeed if it cannot be put in position to go in. (Delta's skills were never in doubt, but the Iranian rescue mission failed because Delta could not be effectively delivered to the American embassy in Teheran.) The importance of having the cooperation of local authorities should also be apparent despite the success of the Djibouti and Entebbe ops without help from the Somalis or Ugandans. In each case, had the authorities cooperated, lives would have been saved.

The necessity for distraction or ruses to gain an instant's edge should have become apparent as well. The use of the drugged food at Djibouti, the fake Idi Amin limo at Entebbe, the F104s at Train 747, the fire on the runway at Mogadishu, and the stun grenades at Princes Gate all illustrate the need for the creative use of distraction at the instant of assault in order to gain a couple of seconds advantage over the terrorists. Split-second timing and outstanding CQB (close quarters battle) skills are, of course, required to capitalize on any slight edge gained.

Though certain basic tenets and tactics can be studied based on these five ops, it would be a mistake to assume that the way to handle a train siege is identical to that of the Dutch Marines, or that an aircraft hijacking should be handled the same way that GSG-9 handled it, or that in order to neutralize an embassy siege one must use tactics identical to those used by the SAS. One can, of course, learn from these operations, but each new hostage situation will have to be individually addressed based on hundreds of considerations which are unique to it. That is one reason the HRU's job is so difficult and why the job requires such a high caliber of men.

CHAPTER 3

Taking Down the S.S. Atlantic Princess

It is sometimes difficult to understand the complexity of a successful hostage rescue operation. The assault, which lasts for only a matter of minutes, of course, grabs one's attention, but the immense amount of preparation (not to mention the years of training) which takes place prior to an assault, is difficult to appreciate. In an attempt to illustrate this complex process, I wish to present a hypothetical terrorist incident and trace the process leading up to a rescue.

THE INCIDENT

The Caribbean cruise ship *S.S. Atlantic Princess* with 227 passengers and 178 crew members aboard pulled into port on the island of Grenada late on the afternoon of 22 June 1987 for a two-day stay. Most of the passengers and a portion of the crew left to visit the island within a couple of hours of docking, while others drifted on and off the liner throughout the evening. Shortly after 11:00 P.M. when 194 passengers and 141 crew members were back on board, a Grenadan taxi pulled up to the dock and disgorged what appeared to be two couples returning from an evening of sight-seeing. As the chatting couples neared the top of the gang plank, however, Czech Skorpian SMGs and CZ-75 pistols were quickly produced as the couples—now revealed as hijackers—rushed the deck, quickly over-powering the crewmen on duty there. Following the initial rush, the "taxi driver" hurried aboard with a large suitcase, which he carried into the lounge where more than 100 passengers were enjoying an evening buffet and drinks. Along with one other hijacker, the "taxi driver's" mission was to immediately secure these passengers as hostages. Producing a detonator from within the suitcase and gripping it in his hand, this terrorist prepared to set off his suitcase, which was full of explosives, should it be necessary.

To gain attention, his partner fired a quick burst of .32 ACP rounds out the lounge doors into the water and announced, "Everyone lie down on the floor. You are now prisoners of the Cuban-Grenadan Joint Liberation Army (CGJLA). Remain calm and cooperate and you will not be harmed. My colleague is holding the deto-nator to enough explosives to blow this ship and all of you into little bits, and he will set it off should we be threatened!"

Meanwhile, two other terrorists proceeded to the communications room, which they quickly secured. The leader of the CGJLA simultaneously welcomed four more heavily armed terrorists aboard. After assigning two of them to positions where they could command the deck, the leader proceeded, with the assistance of the other two new arrivals, to secure the remainder of the ship. Forcing the second mate, who had been the watch officer, to lead the way, these terrorists moved to the ship's fuel storage tanks, where they emplaced addi-tional explosives.

The ship effectively booby-trapped, the captain was awakened and forced to order all crew members on deck, where they were herded together under the AK-47s and grenades carried by the terrorists on watch there. The passengers were all herded together in the main lounge under the guns and explosives of the two terrorists there who had been joined by a third, one of the two women in the terrorist group. Nine terrorists now held 335 hostages under their control, though the number of hostages was somewhat unwieldy. Identification was collected from passengers and crew members by the terrorists as an aid in thinning out the ranks of the hostages and discovering if any of them would make especially good bargaining points (diplomats, for example).

The terrorist leader had also now radioed his initial demands to the office of the harbor master. These demands were simple: the freeing of 20 prominent Latin American Marxist revolutionaries held in various Central and South American countries. All were to be flown to Cuba, as were the terrorists. If the demands were not met within 48 hours, the terrorists would begin to execute the hostages. Should any type of rescue mission be attempted, all hostages would be executed and the ship would be blown up. As a gesture of "Latin solidarity," 124 passengers and crew members carrying Latin American passports were freed. Some other Latins, however, were retained as hostages, obviously to allow more leverage on governments holding some of the terrorists whose release was being demanded.

THE RESPONSE

Representatives of the U.S. State Department, the British government, and the Grenadan government had arrived on the dock area by 2:00 A.M., as had a containment group from the Grenadan police. Though in charge initially, the Grenadan police superintendent on the scene had no way to communicate with the terrorists other than with a bullhorn. A senior superintendent in the harbor master's office was temporarily handling communication with the terrorists via the radio. U.S. State Department negotiators, however, had already been alerted and were preparing to fly to Grenada.

Since jurisdiction for any rescue operation had yet to be decided, both the U.S. Delta and British SAS anti-terrorist units had been alerted for possible deployment to Grenada as well. In case an immediate assault should prove necessary, in fact, one SAS troop had been air-lifted from Belize to Grenada by 0800 on the morning after the hijacking. Though not currently on HRU assignment, all members of this troop had been assigned CRW duties within the previous 12 months. Ensconced in a warehouse near the hijacked liner, this troop followed SOP (Standard Operating Procedure) and pre-pared a standby assault plan should the terrorists begin killing hostages immediately, thereby necessitating an assault. As is normally the case, this standby plan was rather straightforward and called for one four-man team of the troop to act as snipers and take up positions from which they could sweep the decks of the *Atlantic Princess.* Should it prove necessary, when so ordered, they would take out every terrorist target which pre-sented itself. Two of the remaining three teams would mount an assault from the dock while the final four-man team of the troop attempted to board the ship from the sea. Estimates were that at least 50 percent casualties among the assault teams and hostages would result should this scenario take place.

Because of Grenada's ties to Great Britain and because a U.S. ship was involved, a lot of discussion took place as to whether the United States or Great Britain would mount a rescue operation should it be necessary. Fortunately, the two countries work closely on anti-terrorism and it was decided that since Delta had actually trained on the *Atlantic Princess* when it had been docked between cruises at one point and since most of the hostages were Americans, Delta would handle any assault. Of course, the Grenadan government was involved in the discussions and granted permission for Delta to operate on Grenadan soil. The SAS troop already on the scene would remain until Delta could deploy and would stay to lend assistance after Delta's arrival.

The State Department negotiators did their job and kept the situation defused, even managing to convince the terrorists that they still had too many hostages to contend with. Of the remaining 211 hostages, an additional 127 were released by late afternoon, leaving a total of 84 hostages, mostly passengers and mostly Americans. Neither the U.S. nor its Latin American allies wanted to give in to the terrorists, so the negotiators had a difficult assignment—basically, they were to stall as long as possible and convince the terrorists that they were negotiating in good faith. While the negotiations continued, psychiatrists trained to work with hostage negotiators attempted to evaluate the terrorists' states of mind and to determine whether they were likely to carry out their threats. Early indications were that the terrorists meant what they said. On the grounds that it would make communication easier, the negotiators managed to convince the terrorists to allow a telephone line to be run to the *Atlantic Princess.* The value of this line should an assault be necessary was very great since the phone could be rung just prior to the assault, thus occupying at least one or two of the terrorists and locating them for the assault force.

Four members of Delta's intelligence team were on the scene by late morning and had begun to assemble data. Crew members freed earlier were interviewed to determine the location of the terrorists, hostages, and explosives. Some crew members, fortunately, were ex-navy men and thus could give some evaluation of competency of the terrorists by the way they had handled themselves. Two crew members who were interested in firearms managed to identify the weapons carried by the terrorists. Based on the observations by the SAS troop, the identifications were correct. As soon as the second group of hostages was released, the former hostages were scheduled for interviewing.

Back at Fort Bragg, North Carolina, members of

Delta loaded equipment and prepared to deploy to Grenada, while the rest of the intelligence staff began to assemble data on the *Atlantic Princess*, the Grenadan habor and docks, the CGJLA, and the hostages. Blueprints of the *Atlantic Princess* were acquired, and the FBI was asked to gather info and recent photos of the hostages. Because of the time constraints, however, it was assumed that an assault might be necessary before this information arrived. Members of Delta who had served on Grenada during "Operation Urgent Fury" had their brains picked as did members of the 82nd Airborne Division with special knowledge of the dock areas.

Within 20 hours of the takeover of the *Atlantic Princess*, a C-130 carrying 56 members of Delta was touching down at Pearls Airport. Additional members of Delta's intelligence section and other specialists were along, as were a 36-man assault force and six snipers. The assault force included three four-man teams from SEAL (Sea, Air, Land) 6 and six additional four-man assault teams. Since the terrorists were believed to have explosives on board the *Atlantic Princess*, as many men with EOD/demolitions experience as possible were included in the assault teams.

A warehouse near the docks had been appropriated as the headquarters for Delta, and members of the unit were taken there as soon as their equipment could be transferred from the plane to the trucks. Among this equipment were thermal imagers, parabolic microphones, and other high-tech surveillance equipment since locating all nine terrorists was going to be critical to any rescue effort. Using the cover of darkness, Delta operatives skilled in the use of this hardware set up the equipment in windows of a hotel overlooking the harbor.

As the negotiators attempted to keep the terrorists talking, Delta began to consider possible assault tactics. A scale model of the *Atlantic Princess* had been obtained from the cruise line's offices and was being studied, along with the blueprints of the ship. Delta had also taken the responsibility from the SAS troop for an immediate assault should the situation deteriorate rapidly. Constant updates from the negotiations center and the observation points kept the Delta commanding officer (C.O.) apprised of the situation, and pins representing terrorists and hostages were placed on a deck plan of the *Atlantic Princess* on the wall of the command center. Indications from the observers and surveillance devices were that the hostages had now been split into two groups, one still in the lounge and another held in the ship's gymnasium on the lower deck. Three terrorists were assigned to each of these two groups as guards. The primary concern to the HRU was the fact that explosives were located near the fuel tanks and that one terrorist with a detonator was constantly positioned near these explosives. One of the three terrorists guarding the hostages in the lounge also had a detonator for the explosives located there. The two remaining terrorists, including the leader, were usually in the lounge, which is where the telephone had been installed. Since the situation had now gone on for more than 36 hours, it was assumed that fatigue would soon set in amongst the terrorists.

In an attempt to up the ante and increase the pressure on the U.S. government, two hostages were brought out onto the deck at 1020 and were forced to kneel while weapons were placed to their heads. The CGJLA leader then picked up his phone and told the negotiators that he was becoming impatient since no concessions had been made. After talking to the negotiators for nearly ten minutes while the hostages remained under the gun, the leader agreed to stick by his 48-hour deadline before beginning to execute the hostages. He did, however, reiterate that blood would flow once the deadline had passed. The psychiatrist present with the negotiators informed the Delta C.O. that he believed hostages would be executed once the deadline arrived. The President of the United States was also informed, and he ordered

Delta to plan on the assumption that the unit would be sent in if it appeared the hostages would be killed. This gave Delta only a little over 13 hours to finalize preparations for an assault since the deadline would arrive at 0200 the next morning.

Delta snipers had moved into position at six points around the dock area and overlooking the *Atlantic Princess;* they reported that it might be possible to take out the terrorist with the detonator and most of the other terrorists in the lounge through the large "green house" windows. Tentatively, it was decided that top priority would go to the neutralizing of the terrorists with the detonators, even if it meant that other terrorists might have time to begin executing the hostages. It was hoped that in the confusion of an assault the terrorists might hesitate to execute a hostage they'd been in close contact with during the siege. Delta was also counting on a slight edge by striking before the deadline since HRUs have normally not been sent in until a hostage has been killed.

Top priorities in Delta planning now became the neutralization of the terrorists in the gymnasium and of the terrorist with the detonator near the fuel tanks. Another priority was to come up with a diversion. Since the negotiators had reported that the terrorist leader had a particular hatred of President Ronald Reagan, an idea had begun to take form in the Delta C.O.'s mind. The plan would require the cooperation of the President of the United States, but the Delta C.O. had little doubt that the President would help fight terrorism. The President had already tentatively approved a strike before the deadline based on the psychiatrist's evaluation of the terrorists and the Delta C.O.'s recommendation. One real plus for Delta was the size of the *Atlantic Princess;* it would be very difficult for the terrorists to guard the hostages, keep an explosives watch, and observe all possible approaches to the ship once darkness set in. Delta planners began to see possibilities for the successful infiltration of a team aboard the ship after dark. In preparation, the teams from SEAL 6 began to intensively study the deck plans of the ship, planning routes and alternative routes which would lead to the fuel tanks and the gymnasium.

Throughout the remainder of the afternoon, the negotiators attempted to keep the terrorists calm by explaining that negotiations were being carried out at the highest levels to free their fellow terrorists but many of the Latin American governments involved were reluctant to do so. They also told the terrorists that a plane was being made ready for them to fly to Cuba. In the meantime, Delta's plans began to firm up.

Delta would assault as close to 0010 as possible. At 1830, the terrorists were informed that President Reagan would address the terrorists and governments. holding the terrorist prisoners over close-circuit TV and plead for a peaceful solution. The negotiators proposed setting up a giant screen and amplifier on the dock so the terrorists could see the President's sincerity. It was hoped that the terrorist leader would not be able to resist the chance to see the U.S. President he so hated resort to "crawling." After deliberating a short time, the terrorist leader agreed to having the screen set up, though he reiterated that the hostages would die unless his fellow "freedom fighters" were released on schedule. Even before this concession, however, the three teams from SEAL 6 had proceeded to a point across the island and embarked aboard a U.S. Navy craft with their SDVs (Swimmer Delivery Vehicles). Since these teams would make their approach to the *Atlantic Princess* underwater via the SDVs and would need as much time as possible aboard the ship to move carefully into position, it was necessary for them to be released from their mother ship by 2015.

As the large television screen, brought from the U.S. embassy, was being set up on the dock, additional Delta assault teams took up positions inside nearby warehouses and customs sheds. Nevertheless, the closest any of them could get to the ship was about 50 yards. The terrorists had had the gang plank removed earlier so that a simple rush up the gang plank by an anti-terrorist unit was not possible. The assault teams were, however, equipped with a special bridging ladder which could be quickly emplaced for access.

By 2215 the members of SEAL 6 had approached the *Atlantic Princess* from the seaward side and managed to board the ship. Two teams—a total of eight men—gained access to the bowels of the ship through a hatch and began moving cautiously toward their objectives. Two men were assigned to the power plant to cut the ship's power just prior to the assault, two to take out the terrorist assigned to detonate the explosives by the fuel tanks, and four to rescue the hostages held in the gymnasium. The other four-man team remained on deck in hiding. The two SEAL 6 teams moving through the ship took it very slowly and quietly, though they had to cut through one bulkhead with their exothermic torch to gain access to a compartment near the fuel tanks. The two SEALs assigned to take out the terrorist with the detonator near the fuel tanks were both black, and they were dressed similar to two of the terrorists in hopes that, if spotted, the SEAL members might gain an instant while the terrorist hesitated to see whether the men were fellow terrorists. All elements of the assault force were in radio contact, though those aboard the ship communicated only by pushing the talk button on their radios in predetermined codes.

By 2345 the teams in the power plant, near the gymnasium, and near the fuel tanks had all signaled that they were in position. Delta snipers, their rifles equipped with low-light optics, had also signaled that they were in position and ready by 2345. Though it was known that the windows in the lounge were comprised of safety glass, the angle, distance, and bullet being used had been judged a good combination to limit deflection. Two snipers were assigned to take out the terrorist in the lounge with the detonator if he presented himself as a target. The other four would take any terrorists that presented themselves. Each terrorist had been assigned a number, and the windows and doors of the lounge had been assigned letter codes. Hence, a sniper could whisper, "Number three at J" into the microphone to identify whom he had in his sights and where the target was located.

THE ASSAULT

At 2359, Delta was given permission to go in. At 0001, the President began speaking, pleading in fact, with the terrorists over closed-circuit television. The terrorist leader and two others moved onto the upper deck to view the screen, including one who had been guarding the prisoners in the gymnasium on a lower deck. The terrorist with the detonator to the explosives in the lounge also moved to the doorway of the lounge so that he could see and hear the broadcast. Two terrorists remained in the lounge with the hostages, two were in the gymnasium with the hostages that were kept there, and one terrorist was positioned by the explosives located near the fuel tanks.

As the President spoke, the four SEALs crouched in readiness in the shadows on the upper deck, but they were still almost 20 yards from the nearest door or window to the lounge. The key to the operation now rested with the men assigned to take out the terrorists with the detonators. Delta snipers had already indicated that they had the three terrorists on deck, the man with the detonator at the lounge door, and one of the terrorists in the lounge in their sights. At 0008:30, both SEALs near the fuel tanks were in position to place a shot to the base of the skull of the terrorist ready to detonate the explosives by the fuel tanks. So that the terrorists in the gymnasium and on deck would be less likely to hear the shots, the SEALs were armed with their S&W Model Mark 22, Model O pistols. They had been on their own initiative for taking the shot ever since receiving a signal through the receivers worn in their ears that the other terrorist manning the explosives in the lounge was in the crosshairs. They took the shot while it was offered. Even as the terrorist's skull exploded and his fingers released the detonator, their whispered words came over the radio net: "Fuel tanks secured."

Delta's leader then gave the snipers the command, "Kill them!" Six shots rang out as the terrorists on deck and all but one in the lounge were eliminated by 7.62mm bullets traveling at over 2,500 feet per second. All but the terrorist in the lounge were taken with head shots: he was taken with a heart shot since he was standing so that he did not present a head shot. At the sound of the snipers' shots, the four SEALS on deck rushed for the door to the lounge. Simultaneously, the Delta C.O. gave the command to kill the power, and the spotlight on the dock went out, as did the power aboard the ship. Two of the SEAL 6 men heaved stun grenades through two gymnasium doors located 90 degrees from each other, while the remaining two went in low through a third door. Catching the two terrorists disoriented and facing the direction of the first flash, the SEALs quickly acquired their targets with their H&K MP5SD5 SMGs and dropped the terrorists with two bursts of fire.

All of this action on the upper and lower decks had taken place in a very short span of time—not much over a minute—but one terrorist was left in the lounge, and he began to fire his AK-47 wildly into the dark toward the screaming hostages. Members of the SEAL 6 team now bursting into the lounge yelled for the hostages to hit the floor, but amidst the confusion they were having trouble acquiring the target despite his muzzle flashes. Finally, however, the point man on the Delta assault force boarding from the dock burst in behind the terrorist and colandered him at point-blank range.

The SEAL 6 assault team below deck had immediately started moving the hostages toward a stairway to the upper deck, while the other SEAL 6 men below deck secured the rear to make sure no terrorists from the deck above could take them by surprise. As soon as they received communication that the upper deck was secured, they ushered their charges onto the deck and toward the gang plank, which was quickly re-emplaced. Once on the dock, the hostages were herded together and covered by members of Delta's intelligence section until it could be ascertained that none had brought any booby traps off the ship nor had cooperated with the terrorists. Even before the power had been restored, the assault team members on the deck began herding uninjured passengers or those wounded who could walk toward the gang plank as well. Since no one was sure whether the ship had been booby-trapped, it was necessary to clear it as soon as possible. During the wild firing in the lounge, two hostages had been killed and nine others were wounded, three seriously. One SEAL had been slightly wounded in the lounge as well. Medical personnel standing by on the docks dealt with the injured once the deck was secured.

The assault had been an operational and tactical success, marked by the television participation of the American President.

ANALYSIS

A few things should be pointed out regarding this hypothetical rescue. It must be understood that the scenario I have presented was an extremely complicated one, and, in reality, gaining clandestine access to the ship and coordinating the various aspects would have been extremely difficult. I have also glossed over certain details regarding how the operation would have gone down, both for conciseness and, in some cases, for security. In the scenario I have set up, time was a key factor; therefore, certain aspects of planning and rehearsal for an assault had to be compressed. There was no time, for example, for Delta to practice assaults on a sister ship to the *Atlantic Princess* or to get photos of the terrorists and hostages to study for rapid target acquisition and decision-making during the assault when a "shoot, don't shoot," decision must instantly be made. I have also not gone into great detail concerning the technology and weapons involved since many of these items are described elsewhere. Certain things were included to illustrate specific points: For example, the fact that the SAS was first on the scene illustrates the need to establish jurisdiction and cooperation between top notch HRUs (in this case, the SAS and Delta).

This chapter is included in *The Rescuers* in order to illustrate the immense complexity of carrying out a successful assault to rescue hostages. I have also tried to show some of the tactics and equipment likely to be used and some of the difficulties likely to be encountered. The bottom line, though, is that I created the scenario; I created the assault; and I created the conclusion. Obviously, I was in much more control of events than any HRU could be when they have to "take down" an objective. (The disastrous Egyptian assault at Malta and the Colombian assault on the Justice Palace graphically illustrate how easily things can go wrong in the real world.)

CHAPTER 4

European Anti-Terrorist Units

Although Israel certainly ranks among the pioneers in forming special anti-terrorist units, European countries which had experienced hijackings, kidnappings, and other terrorist acts during the late 1960s and early Seventies saw the need for highly trained hostage rescue forces more than a decade ago. Pioneered by Great Britain, West Germany and France, they began forming and training units especially to deal with the terrorist threat. Other countries followed the lead of the larger Western European countries and formed their own military or police units to counter the threat of terrrorism.

Few, however, could afford the expense necessary to maintain a unit on a full-time basis just to deal with terrorist acts, thus diluting the effort to some extent as such units began to be used as sky marshals, VIP protective forces, area security personnel, etc. As long as the unit was kept together and a constant training schedule was adhered to, though, its skills remained sharp. If, however, the unit was split up and assigned other duties, being called together only periodically to train for its anti-terrorist role, then its skills normally declined or did not reach the level of such units as GSG-9 or the SAS.

The very fact that acts of terrorism in Western Europe have declined substantially from their peak in the 1970s can perhaps illustrate the success of the Western European anti-terrorist effort. Excellent cooperation between many of the units themselves has also helped combat the terrorist threat in Europe as the various agencies have shared training, technology, and intelligence. It is also noteworthy that four of the five classic anti-terrorist operations previously analyzed were carried out by Western European HRUs. During the later Seventies, the Europeans were targets of both internal and external terrorist threats and responded accordingly by allocating manpower and other resources to countering the threat. The following discussion of the various European units will attempt to show how the organization, training, tactics, and equipment of each unit have evolved and how each unit has fared when called upon to "go in" against terrorists. To protect members of the HRUs and the hostages they might have to rescue in the future, certain tactics and equipment will not be mentioned or will be covered only sketchily. Surprise remains an important weapon in the anti-terrorist arsenal and though most readers should find this chapter and others interesting and informative, they should never doubt that any good HRU has a lot of tricks not to be found in this work.

SPECIAL AIR SERVICE

Britain's Special Air Service (SAS) was not really formed as an anti-terrorist unit but as a military raiding and intelligence-gathering unit. During the last three decades, however, the SAS has been used primarily against Communist insurgencies and on other types of "anti-terrorist" operations. By the late 1960s, the SAS was providing training teams to teach close quarters battle skills to the bodyguards of foreign heads of state friendly to Britain and in a few cases, such as for the Sultan of Oman, were actually providing bodyguards themselves. Beginning in this period, 15 to 20 members of the SAS were assigned to study terrorism and develop tactics to combat hijackers or other terrorists. Since 1969, members of the SAS have also been deployed to Northern Ireland, including during more recent years an HRU/strike unit known as the "House-Assault Group."

As the terrorist threat became more prevalent in the mid-Seventies, however, the SAS began to devote more men to anti-terrorist duties until eventually one full squadron of 78 men was assigned. This remains the normal strength of the CRW (Counter Revolutionary Warfare) Squadron today. Note that "CRW Squadron" is the term normally used by the press, but within the SAS this unit is normally called the "SP Team" (Special Projects Team). The SP Team does not retain that duty indefinitely as each of the SAS's squadrons performs this function on rotation, normally for a six-month period. Because of the SAS's rigorous selection process and effective training program, this system works quite well and establishes a large pool of trained manpower that can instruct friendly nations in HRU tactics or carry out this mission itself in Northern Ireland or elsewhere a squadron might be assigned.

The CRW Squadron is broken into four operational troops of one officer and 15 other ranks. Each of these teams is broken further into four-man operating units. For assaults, this four-man unit operates in pairs as two-man teams. Normally, each of the operational troops is divided into a containment group which will include snipers and surveillance specialists and an assault group. In practice, most members of the operational troop can perform virtually any of the functions. Backing up the CRW Squadron is the SAS's small but highly efficient Ops Research Unit which has developed many special-purpose devices for anti-terrorist usage, the most well-known of which is the stun grenade. Special assault ladders and light mounts for weapons have also come out of the Ops Research Unit. The SP Team, in fact, has a large inventory of special high-tech equipment and vehicles, including vans with hinge-mounted ladders for rapid second-story entry, diverse night optics, and other surveillance items such as thermal imagers and endoscopes.

Many of the skills normally taught to anti-terrorist units—such as parachuting, scuba, mountaineering, rapelling, hand-to-hand combat, field medicine, marksmanship, communications, and demolitions—are skills members of the SAS have normally already acquired by the time they are assigned to CRW duties. One of the keystones to the SAS's effectiveness at anti-terrorist duties is its intensive firearms training program which not only stresses marksmanship but also tactics. The SAS CQB House ("Killing House") was originally developed during the days of training bodyguards but has been adapted for HRU assault training. The basic CQB shooting course lasts for six weeks during which 1,200 to 1,500 rounds minimum are expended. Far more rounds will later be fired by members of the SP Team to keep their skills sharp.

Shooting on the move and from unconventional positions, rapid magazine changes, malfunction clearance drills, rapid target acquisition, and exact shot placement are all practiced until they become automatic. Another SAS innovation is the use of members of the SP Team as "hostages" during live-fire tactical exercises. Scenarios are often set up with hostages very close to the terrorist targets. Double taps are used with the handgun and three-round bursts with the SMG to assure dropping the adversary, and head shots are practiced intensively in case this is the only target offered. Instinctive point shooting is stressed until members of the SAS become masters at it.

Scenarios are set up by the SAS to duplicate all types of possible hostage situations—aboard trains, airliners, ships, and in various types of buildings.

The SAS has very good relations with most other

Western HRUs, especially the U.S. Delta unit, West Germany's GSG-9, the Royal Dutch Marines, and Spain's GEO. Relations are not all that good with the Israelis since the SAS is very clannish and has a long memory about such incidents as the letter bomb from Jewish terrorists which killed the brother of former SAS officer Roy Farran. As a result, the SAS still views the Israelis with a certain amount of distrust. Therefore, contacts with the Israelis are usually through GSG-9.

The primary assault weapon for the SAS is the H&K MP5, which it adopted after seeing its performance with GSG-9 at Mogadishu. Prior to that time, the SP Team had assaulted with the MAC-10 but was unhappy with its accuracy due to its high cyclic rate. As its secondary arm (primary in certain scenarios such as clearing a single confined room) the SAS uses the Browning Hi-Power. Accuracy International builds the SAS SP Team's sniper's rifle in three configurations—"Hard Kill" in 7.62 for 300+ meters, "Soft Kill" in .243 Winchester for under 300 meters, and "Silent Kill" in suppressed form. Formerly, the SAS used the TIKKA .22-250 sniper's rifle. Remington 870 shotguns are used to take out door hinges or for certain close-quarter combat scenarios.

The SAS's assault garb is now well-known due to the fact that its operation at Princes Gate was televised. SAS members wear an anti-flash hood (often made from an NBC suit), with a gas mask and black utilities. The ballistic vest worn at Princes Gate was the BCME Variable Armor. Others, including Silent Partner-types, are reportedly available. Currently, the SP Team is using a one-piece black Nomex suit with an integral hood and elbow/knee stress points reinforced with Kevlar. Their well-known drop holster rides low on the leg with spare mag pouches for the MP5 worn low on the other leg. A spare Hi-Power magazine is often worn on the strong-side wrist to be readily available for a rapid mag change. Extension 20-round magazines are often carried in the Hi-Power. The gas mask and anti-flash hood (or balaclava) not only add to the fearsomeness of the assault team's appearance (thus perhaps giving them a split-second edge) but also aid unit members to instantly identify one another during an assault. The fact that the gas mask is already in place saves valuable time, too, should it be necessary to deploy CS gas, especially since SAS stun grenades often include CS gas as well as the "Flash, Bang!" components. Communications (commo) equipment is worn beneath the mask.

The SAS's most famous operational deployment was, of course, the Princes Gate assault, which was covered previously. There have, however, been other deployments. In 1972, for example, SAS and SBS (Special Boat Squadron) men parachuted into the sea and boarded the QE II in response to a bomb threat. January 1975 saw the SAS deployed when an Iranian hijacked an airliner from Manchester. He wanted to fly to Paris, which is where he was fooled into believing he had landed when, in actuality, the airliner came down in Essex. There, an SAS team awaited him, quickly ended the hijacking, and took him alive. In December 1975, the SAS was employed once again when four members of the IRA were barricaded in Balcombe Street. When the IRA members heard over the radio that the SAS was prepared to move in, they surrendered.

The SAS's expertise has been called upon more than once by Britain's allies. In May 1977, members of the SAS were sent to offer stun grenades to the Dutch Marines for the assault on Train 747. When they returned, these SAS men helped set up practice assaults on trains for the SAS CRW Squadron. Then, in October 1977, two SAS men aided GSG-9 with stun grenades during the assault in Mogadishu. The SAS had also been available when the hijacked Lufthansa airliner was on the ground in Dubai to act as liaisons since the SAS has good contacts there. Should an assault in Dubai have been necessary and GSG-9 not have been given approval to carry it out, the SAS was even prepared to train the Dubai Royal Guard in assault tactics prior to a rescue attempt.

In 1978, members of the SAS were sent to Italy to aid Italian anti-terrorist units after the kidnapping of Premier Aldo Moro. Reportedly, the SAS also gave a certain amount of assistance to the U.S. Delta unit prior to their mission into Iran during April 1980. Finally, the SAS CRW specialists burst into world prominence when their assault on the Iranian embassy in London was televised on 5 May 1980.

Since that time, the SAS has continued to provide bodyguards to certain British officials in high-threat situations, especially diplomats. In one case an SAS man in Central America reportedly foiled an attempted kidnapping of a British diplomat. When Libyan "diplomats" fired on a crowd, killing a British policewoman in April 1984, the SAS was also reportedly ready to "go in" if necessary. The SP Team remains on alert at Hereford, ready for immediate deployment should they be needed. High-speed autos and other vehicles as well as aircraft are available to take them where needed, and the SAS remains a formidable deterrent to terrorist acts against Britain.

Other British Anti-Terrorist Units

Although the SAS is the primary national HRU for Great Britain, certain other units with anti-terrorist missions must also be mentioned. Comacchio Company of the Royal Marines is charged with anti-terrorist responsibility for the North Sea oil rigs. This 300- to 400-man company has a large contingent of swimmer canoeists (SBS) assigned and has carried out numerous practice assaults on rigs from choppers, small boats, and underwater via submarine or parachute insertion.

The SBS (Special Boat Squadron) also has certain other anti-terrorist responsibilities involving ships and certain shore installations and works closely with the SAS to coordinate in those areas where their missions overlap. The SBS also works closely with Scandinavian units with similar North Sea missions.

The Parachute Regiment receives at least a limited amount of anti-terrorist training and has carried out joint training with the U.S. Army Rangers on rescues.

The London Metropolitan Police's D11 unit should also be mentioned. The Met's equivalent of a U.S. police SWAT Team, D11 is formed with the Met's firearms instructors as its basis. D11 is trained primarily for containment and as snipers, but some members are also trained for assaults in situations which do not seem to merit calling in the SAS. It should be noted that the SAS will normally only get involved in "political" situations and not criminal ones.

Controversy has surrounded D11's armament, especially with SMGs. D11 reportedly acquired some Sterling SMGs quite a few years ago but kept them secret. Some semi-auto H&K MP5A2s were acquired, and it is possible that this is the version which can be switched to full auto with a key. Since D11's primary responsibility has often been to provide snipers/countersnipers, it could be argued that the L39A1 7.62mm sniper's rifles with which the unit is equipped is the most important weapon. For shorter range "sniping," the H&K 93 in 5.56mm is available. Reportedly, other rifles, including the Parker Hale and the Enfield Enforcer, have been used as well for sniping in the past. D11's basic handgun has been the S&W Model 10 revolver. However, operationally D11 normally uses either the Browning Hi-Power, S&W Model 19 .357 Mag, or S&W Model 29 .44 Mag. Other specialized armament or assault equipment includes Remington 870 shotguns, tear gas guns, stun grenades, and ballistic vests. D11 wears blue berets to distinguish themselves. The unit also fields outstanding police pistol teams, one indication of the high level of their shooting skill.

In addition to containment duties prior to the SAS assault at Princes Gate, D11 has been called out to deal with various hostage situations during the last few years.

One recent call-out in Northolt, Middlesex, resulted in a great deal of criticism of D11, though in actuality much of the criticism should have been leveled at the Divisional Commander who refused to make a decision to send in D11 and who issued orders that the hostage-taker should not be shot. After one hostage had been killed, D11 was allowed to assault, though its entry tactics, use of flash bangs, speed of entry, and marksmanship did leave something to be desired. Certainly, the loss of surprise was a contributing factor, though. One of three rounds fired from a Browning Hi-Power took the hostage-taker in the head and ended the situation.

Because of the situation in Northern Ireland, an SAS "House-Assault Group" to act as an HRU/assault team and Special Forces NITIC Teams to carry out covert ops have been deployed. The RUC (Royal Ulster Constabulary) is, however, now deploying two units of its own—an HRU similar to D11 and a covert ops/surveillance unit known as E4-Alpha.

GSG-9

The death of 11 Israeli Olympic athletes at the hands of Black September terrorists graphically illustrated to West German authorities their lack of preparedness to deal with hostage situations. As a result, Hans-Dietrich Genscher, the Federal Minister of the Interior, was given permission to form a special unit to combat terrorists. For various reasons, including reluctance to form any type of military elite which might bring back memories of the SS, it was decided to form the new group within the Federal Border Police (the Bundesgrenzchutz), which were paramilitary and had national authority. Designated Grenzchutzgruppe 9 (GSG-9), this new unit had an authorized strength of 188 men.

The new unit was stationed at St. Augustin just outside Bonn so it would be near the seat of government for the Federal Republic. Though primarily intended to

act as the national HRU against terrorists, it was foreseen that GSG-9 might undertake other special tasks
such as guarding VIPs in high-risk situations, providing
special security for German embassies likely to be
attacked, or providing security at sensitive installations
in extreme situations. Appointed to command GSG-9
was Ulrich Wegener, a 15-year veteran of the border
police and an expert on terrorism. Even before assuming command of GSG-9, Wegener had trained with the
FBI and the Israelis, but after assuming command of the
new anti-terrorist unit he strengthened his ties with the
Israelis even more. Reportedly, in fact, Wegener accom-
panied the Israelis on the Entebbe Raid in 1976.
Wegener began forming his special unit during late 1972
and by early '73, it was operational. To help build esprit
de corps within GSG-9, the green beret was adopted in
1973.

GSG-9 was originally organized into three strike units
backed up by other support units, including an HQ,
communications and intelligence unit, engineer unit,
weapons unit, research and equipment unit, maintenance and supply unit, and training unit. In 1983 a
fourth strike unit was added. Each of these strike units
was made up of 30 men, broken into a command
section and five SETs (Specialein-satztrupp). Strength
of the strike units has reportedly since been increased
to 42 men. The five-man SET is the GSG-9 basic operational unit and can be deployed in various modular
increments. SETs can function as assault sections or
sniper sections. On special assignments such as VIP
protection, a five-man SET often operates independ-
ently. GSG-9 has found, as have many other special
units, that small units such as the SETs offer better
command and control, better mobility, and greater
flexibility. In a hostage situation, it is the SETs which
actually go in, while the sniper SETs take out a terrorist
or terrorists at a distance should a shot offer itself.

Since intelligence is a key part of anti-terrorist operations, GSG-9 is hooked directly into the giant computer

system in Wiesbaden known as The Komissar. The Komissar keeps track of world terrorist groups, especially those which have operated in the Federal Republic, and compiles information about their methods, organization, doctrine, membership, movements, and other factors. GSG-9 is also supported by the district BGS helicopter wing which is based next to the GSG-9 barracks. This unit works very closely with GSG-9 during training and is familiar with the various ways it might be employed for tactical insertions. This is an excellent system and, in effect, virtually gives GSG-9 an integral airmobile arm.

To be selected for GSG-9, the aspiring border guard must be an exceptional individual—both physically and mentally. To even apply for GSG-9 the candidate must have served 2 1/2 years in the BGS with a good record. After application, he must then go through a three-day initial selection process consisting of a psychological aptitude test, an endurance and shooting test, a physical-fitness test (including stress factors), an intelligence and general knowledge test, and a medical examination. Also included is an interview with GSG-9 officers. This preliminary process weeds out about two-thirds of the prospective members of GSG-9.

For those who make it through the initial selection, there is a five-month initial training phase, which about another 10 percent normally fail. During this phase, physical training and the development of certain technical skills are stressed, especially shooting and the martial arts. The next, and final, training module lasts three months and emphasizes specialized skills, particularly teamwork and assault tactics as part of a SET.

Firearms training in GSG-9 is with handguns, sniper's rifles, and SMGs. Three half-days and one night per week are devoted to shooting practice within GSG-9. Included within this training are a large number of tactical scenarios which use mockups of airplanes, trains, ships, embassies, or other likely operational targets. To facilitate training, GSG-9 has a $9,000,000 underground range at St. Augustin, which even includes aircraft mockups. The GSG-9 trooper also learns to use and recognize foreign weapons, especially those (such as the AK-47 and Czech M-61) which are popular with terrorists, so that he knows the capabilities of weapons he may be up against and also learns how to turn the terrorist's own weapons on him should they fall into GSG-9 hands. Other shooting skills which are constantly practiced include weak-handed shooting, malfunction clearance drills, tactical reloads, use of cover, firing under assault conditions (including after use of stun grenades or breaching charges), precise shot placement in hostage scenarios, and firing from vehicles or helicopters or while rappelling.

Although this extensive firearms training, along with hand-to-hand skills, makes a GSG-9 member an efficient killer when he has to be, GSG-9's philosophy is to attempt to take prisoners if possible. As a result, great stress is placed on the martial arts and the use of the SMG or rifle as a nonlethal weapon in hand-to-hand combat; GSG-9 members become very efficient at wielding the butts of their MP5s! Among other skills learned by GSG-9 members are HALO, LALO, and other types of parachuting; scuba; demolitions and explosive ordnance disposal (EOD); communications; first aid; skiing and mountaineering; chopper insertions (including abseiling); high-speed driving; police science; and law. A lot of time is also spent studying airport operations and learning many airport jobs, including pilot and steward, so the GSG-9 commando can infiltrate a hijacked airliner by passing as an airport employee or crew members.

One of the hardest tasks GSG-9 faces is keeping the edge necessary to perform its mission if called upon. As a result, 50 to 70 hours per week are spent training, and twice yearly each member of the unit must pass a qualification test to show that his skills are still up to standard. Both to increase knowledge and to offer a change of pace, members of the unit do exchange training with such units as the U.S. FBI and Delta, British SAS, French GIGN, and Israeli "Sayaret Matkal." Other anti-terrorist specialists hold GSG-9 in such high esteem that there are almost always members of other such units training with GSG-9.

GSG-9 takes advantage of the technological expertise available in the Federal Republic and deploys some of the most sophisticated weapons and equipment available to carry out its mission. Originally, GSG-9 used S&W Model 36 or 60 revolvers or H&K P7 or P9S autos, but operationally at Mogadishu the Chief's Special proved to lack the necessary stopping power. As a result, though the P9S and P7 remain standard arms, the Model 36/60 has been replaced by the Model 19 .357 Magnum with 2 1/2 inch barrel. Members of the unit are, in fact, given some freedom in choosing their handgun, though almost all use either the Model 19, P7, or P9S. Model 29 S&W .44 Magnum revolvers and P9S .45 ACP autos are available as well should more stopping power be needed, though with the special ammo available to GSG-9 the .357 and 9x19 rounds both have plenty of punch. The basic GSG-9 SMG is the H&K MP5, with the suppressed MP-5SD seeing a lot of use. The MP-5K and other variations of the system are also available. The MP-5K is especially useful when GSG-9 members are assigned to VIP protection for which they have special briefcases with MP-5Ks inside; squeezing a lever built into the handle of the briefcase fires the weapon. For night operations the various MP5s can be equipped with the ZPP or other low-light optics.

For precision shooting at long range, GSG-9 has an impressive armory of sniper's rifles and special-purpose optics. For many years, the Mauser Model 66 bolt action in 7.62mmx51 caliber and with a Zeiss telescopic sight has been used by GSG-9. More recently, the H&K PSG-1 and the Walther WA2000 with various types of special optics have been used. The H&K SG1 in 7.62mm x51 equipped with an Eltro infrared scope is also in the GSG-9 armory.

Should a shotgun be needed for blasting off hinges during an entry or for anti-personnel use, the H&K 502 is used. The H&K G8 light machine gun with 4X scope provides heavy firepower for very special circumstances.

Among other special GSG-9 equipment is the Bristol armored vest, GSG-9's standard body armor. Weighing in at 19 pounds, the Bristol vest is obviously not among the more lightweight body armors. Considering its ability to stop a .44 Magnum round at point-blank range and the high state of physical fitness of members of GSG-9 which enables them to carry this weight with little effect on their maneuvering ability, it's a good choice. For abseiling, the IKAR type AS1 rig is used.

To get the SETs into action and to make use of the excellent GSG-9 high-speed driving training, high-performance Mercedes Benz 280SE sedans (with a top speed of 125 MPH+) and a battery of sophisticated commo equipment give GSG-9 rapid pursuit and deployment capability over the autobahns. Of course, GSG-9 can also be deployed via helicopter or other methods. Helicopter tactics are often coordinated with auto pursuits. GSG-9 snipers also practice pouring fire into the engine compartment of fleeing vehicles and are very adept at bringing them to a stop. From choppers, GSG-9 men can perform the same tactic by pouring fire from above into the engine compartment with their MP5s.

During GSG-9's early years there was a certain amount of jealousy concerning the amount of money spent on the new unit and questions about its utility, especially since many of the state police forces had formed their own HRUs. This all changed on 17 October 1977, however, when GSG-9 went into action at Mogadishu Airport in Somalia to rescue 91 hostages aboard a hijacked Lufthansa airliner.

The success at Mogadishu brought GSG-9 national and international fame with more than 40 countries (including Somalia, Saudi Arabia, and Singapore) requesting assistance in forming their own anti-terrorist units along GSG-9 lines. Even the SAS asked Ulrich Wegener's advice prior to their classic operation at Princes Gate.

Early in 1979 GSG-9 found itself involved in preventive duties as members of the unit advised on strengthening the defenses at embassies in Teheran and Beirut. GSG-9 men have also seen use on special assignments at some Latin American embassies. The number of threats against government officials and NATO officers stationed in Germany has caused GSG-9 to become even more involved in VIP protection in the last few years as well. In addition to providing actual protective teams, GSG-9 has trained special units of the U.S. Military Police for VIP protective assignments for NATO officers.

In 1979 GSG-9's strength was increased to 219 men and Col. Wegener was promoted to Brigadier General in 1981, when he became the commander of BGS West. Though GSG-9 still falls under Wegener's command, the new unit commander became LTC Klaus Blatte, who was succeeded in 1982 by LTC Uwe Dee.

Though it has not been used again on a full-scale international operation such as at Mogadishu, GSG-9 has kept its edge by carrying out sensitive protective assignments and reportedly carrying at least one unpublicized surgical mission. GSG-9 also played a key role in apprehending two RAF terrorists at an arms cache in November 1982 where the GSG-9 men had set up a stakeout. GSG-9 has also continued to provide training assistance to other countries and has thus aided many of West Germany's foreign policy aims by making friends in the Third World.

SEK

At about the same time that GSG-9 was formed, many major German cities formed their own SEKs (Speziale-insatz Kommando), which would be similar to an American SWAT team. These units received training in sniping/countersniping, rapelling, assault tactics, combat shooting, breaching tactics, hand-to-hand combat, and VIP protection. These units have been used primarily to carry out dangerous arrests, provide perimeter security at important VIP gatherings and security at important government installations, to rescue hostages in non-"political" situations, and to provide VIP protection. Normally, these units operate in three- to five-man teams for assault and other duties.

Armament for the SEKs includes P5, P6, and P7 9mm autos but .357 Magnum revolvers, normally Smith & Wessons, are used in some cases. The standard SMG is the H&K MP5, while the Mauser 66, Steyr SSG, and H&K SG1 are relatively common sniper's rifles. The newer H&K PSG-1 is also being used by some SEKs.

In addition to large cities, the German federal states often have their own SEKs, too. Bavaria, for example, has a very well-trained one. Among the cities with especially competent SEKs are West Berlin, Frankfurt, and Stuttgart.

GIGN

By 1971, France's Gendarmerie Nationale, a 60,000- strong militarized police force under the control of the Ministry of Defense, was already considering the formation of a special anti-terrorist unit. The takeover of the Saudi Arabian embassy in Paris in September 1973, following the murder of Israeli Olympic athletes in Munich during 1972, resulted in the implementation of these plans in November 1973, when GIGN—the Groupement D'Intervention De La Gendarmerie National- ale—was formed.

In these early days, GIGN was split into two com- mands—GIGN 1 at Maisons-Alfort just outside Paris and GIGN 4 at Mont-de-Marsan. GIGN 1 had responsi- bility for northern France and GIGN 4 for southern France. GIGN 1, however, was commanded by the unit's commanding officer, Lt. Prouteau, and thus by default became the premier unit. Prouteau's dual responsibility included command of all 15 men originally assigned to GIGN (three five-man teams) and the operational control of both GIGN units.

In 1976, however, the two commands merged to form one cohesive unit under Prouteau, who had been promoted to captain. As GIGN's responsibilities grew, so did its strength; by 1979, the unit had two officers and 40 NCOs. The basic strike unit of GIGN was at that time a 12-man team of NCOs. As of 1979, there were three of these teams, each composed of a team commander, dog handler, and two five-man intervention forces. When operational, one of the two officers or the senior NCO would normally take overall command. One of the three teams was on alert status 24 hours a day for deployment anywhere in France or the world within half an hour. By 1984 GIGN had been expanded once again to four 12-man teams of NCOs and four officers. The unit commander as of 1984 was Capt. Phillipe Masslen.

In addition to serving as France's national HRU, GIGN is also charged with transporting extremely dangerous criminals, providing VIP protection at very high levels in very high-threat situations, dealing with prison sieges, and providing security for highly sensitive installations (such as nuclear power plants) should a criminal or terrorist threat seem likely.

GIGN candidates are all volunteers drawn from the Gendarmerie Nationale who have successfully made it through a preliminary screening and through an interview with the unit CO. During this interview the candidate's poise and dedication are evaluated, and he is made aware of the hardships involved in serving with GIGN. Those candidates making it through these preliminaries join about 100 others for the physical portion of the selection process, which includes tests of endurance, agility, and marksmanship. The physical tests include an eight-kilometer run with full combat pack in under 40 minutes, a 50-meter swim in under 15 seconds, a seven-meter rope climb in under seven seconds, and tests of rappelling ability and general coordination. Reportedly, tests of courage such as going one-on-one against an attack-trained dog or against a GIGN martial arts expert are included in the physical testing. Underwater swimming tests are also included. GIGN places great emphasis on marksmanship; though the firearms training is excellent, the candidate is expected to already possess basic expertise. Minimum shooting scores deemed acceptable for admission are 70 out of 100 at 25 meters with the handgun and 75 out of 100 at 200 meters with the rifle.

Surprise tests—sickener factors as the SAS calls them—are thrown into the tests at various points to evaluate the candidate's ability to think on his feet and to weed out those without the "heart" for GIGN. These various selection tests last about a week, at the end of which normally only one man will be selected for full GIGN training. Once selected, however, he can look forward to an eight-month probation while he is trained and assimilated onto an operational team. The training he will face is constant, rigorous, and diverse. It is not just the recruit who undergoes it, either; all GIGN members train constantly to maintain the keen edge needed should they be deployed. And, of course, GIGN has to be ready for deployment at any time.

Physical training continues as long as a man remains with GIGN. Running includes long-distance, cross-country runs to build endurance, along with sprints. Calisthenics, weight training, and martial arts combine to build strength and coordination. Both karate and judo are practiced full contact and all out so the GIGN man will react instantly and unflinchingly in action. Many members of the unit are, in fact, black belts. Disarming and rapid neutralization techniques are especially emphasized during martial arts training. GIGN members also receive ski and mountain training at schools such as that of the 11th Parachute Division at Bareges. This training, of course, aids in physical fitness but also enables the GIGN man to be ready for operations in the Alps or elsewhere in snow or on heights.

Although all anti-terrorist units stress swimming ability, GIGN puts even greater stress on it, and all members of the unit are qualified as "Nageurs de Combat" (combat swimmers). In addition to being able to swim 50 meters rapidly, the GIGN man is expected to be able to carry out a long-distance swim while pulling a 75-kilo dummy (representing someone being rescued). Up to four hours per week are spent on underwater swimming training, both with scuba gear and free diving. One GIGN technique to develop confidence in one's swimming skills is to require a man to dive to the bottom of the Seine and lie waiting on the bottom in the murky water under the barge passage while these mammoth vessels pass only a few meters overhead. This exercise develops patience and confidence which may prove necessary for the GIGN assault force should it have to infiltrate a target underwater. Such an exercise also teaches the diver to avoid disorientation, claustrophobia, and panic.

GIGN free-diving training also includes some difficult exercises, one of which requires the swimmer to dive to the bottom of an 18-meter deep ditch, read a question on a tablet, write the answer with a water-proof pen, and then return to the surface—all without breathing apparatus. This exercise not only develops endurance but also the ability to stay calm and think. All diving techniques are designed to allow the GIGN man to infiltrate a hijacked ocean liner, yacht, or beach-side hotel while remaining undetected. As a result, members of GIGN even learn such sophisticated combat swimming techniques as locking in and out of a submerged submarine and use of "closed circuit" scuba equipment (which does not give off the bubbles that might betray the swimmer's presence).

All members of GIGN receive parachute training at the French jump school at Pau and wear their parachute wings proudly on their right breasts. Many members are commando qualified, too. Since they must remain on jump status, each member of GIGN makes five jumps per year, normally including at least one "wet" jump into the water in scuba gear.

Just as it is one of the foremost advocates of scuba training among big league HRUs, GIGN stresses rappelling skill even more than most, and virtually all HRUs stress rappelling. GIGN considers this skill to be one of the most important methods for gaining entrance to a terrorist-controlled building and thus practices rope work constantly. GIGN members become very adept at rappelling into shooting position and then firing very accurately with their revolvers one-handed. The "pendulum" technique of entering a room by swinging through a window—normally in conjunction with other members of the unit breaching the door—is another rappelling technique in the GIGN repertoire.

Helicopter insertion techniques such as jumping directly to the ground, a building top, or into the water; rappelling or parachuting from a helicopter; or winching from a helicopter are all practiced either separately or as part of tactical scenarios. Using the rappel from a helicopter, the GIGN commando is expected to make the slide in under seven seconds; six is preferred. Normally, GIGN practices helicopter insertions, especially rappelling, at least once a month.

Since motor vehicles may have to be used to take GIGN into action or in a pursuit, high-speed driving training takes place at Le Mans. This, of course, stands any GIGN man assigned as a VIP driver in good stead as well. The Citroen is GIGN's primary vehicle.

Although GIGN follows a police philosophy and prefers to avoid deadly force if possible when it is called for, the GIGN policy is that the target has to be instantly neutralized. Exact shot placement is, therefore, stressed so that the terrorist can be stopped before he can harm a hostage. With the revolver, the GIGN man is expected to be able to place a shot exactly on a moving target at ranges out to 25 meters within two seconds.

Within five seconds, each man is expected to be able to successfully engage six targets at 25 meters. Unlike some units who have specialized sharpshooters, each GIGN man is expected to be expert with the rifle. At 200 meters with the rifle, he is expected to be able to achieve a minimum score of 93 out of 100, but most GIGN members do much better: 98 out of 100 with or without telescopic sights being about the norm at 200 meters. To train for the rapid shots necessary in some scenarios, some rifle exercises require the shooter to align the sights and fire in under two seconds. Standard GIGN rifle practice takes place at ranges out to 300 meters, but exercises are sometimes set up which require even longer shots. Each GIGN member normally averages at least two hours per day on the range, including quite a bit of night shooting, and on the average fires more than 9,000 rounds per year through his revolver and 3,000 rounds per year through his rifle. "His" is the correct term, too, since each GIGN man is issued his personal rifle so that he will know it perfectly should he have to use it operationally.

Some additional range time is spent with the SMG, fighting shotgun, likely terrorist weapons, and various other special weapons, including a sophisticated slingshot which fires steel balls and would be used by GIGN for a silent kill. Suppressed firearms are also available to perform the same function. Some range sessions also include specialized exercises within mock-ups of aircraft cabins and from within or firing at moving vehicles. Shooting under unfavorable conditions (such as in a room filled with CS gas or immediately after pitching in a stun grenade) is also stressed during scenario training. Engagement speed is built through man-on-man dueling in which two members of the unit try to see who can engage a target most rapidly. GIGN combat swimmers even receive training in engaging a target with their revolvers as soon as they break the surface. In addition to building great shooting skill, GIGN firearms training is designed to eliminate any tendency to "cowboy" with firearms.

Originally, GIGN members were armed with 9mm auto pistols as their basic handgun, but these have been replaced with the Manurhin 73 .357 Magnum revolver, a very reliable and accurate French revolver which entered service in 1974. For operational use, the Model 73 with 5 1/4 inch barrel and adjustable sights is preferred; when concealment is important, though, three-inch models are available. As a backup handgun, some members of the unit choose a large-magazine capacity 9mm auto, such as the MAB PAP Mle F1. At least a few GIGN men reportedly carry a S&W Model 29 .44 Magnum. To ensure reliability, even when fired by GIGN combat swimmers, special .357 Magnum ammo is loaded for GIGN by Norma. When loading a GIGN contract, in fact, Norma shuts down a normal production line and sets up a special one with enhanced quality control, especially in the areas of consistency and waterproofing. Although SMGs are available for assault, GIGN normally thinks of the Manurhin as its assault weapon.

Each GIGN man has also been issued an FR-F1 sniper's rifle (reportedly being upgraded to FR-F2s). The FR-F1 or F2 is a 7.62mm bolt action with a free-floating barrel, butt spacers, bipod, flash suppressor, and other aids for accurate shooting. Various optics are available for day or night shooting. H&K SG1 selective-fire rifles with sophisticated optics have also been used.

When GIGN uses an SMG, it is normally the MP5A3, MP5SD, or MP5K, depending on the situation. Riot guns and other sound-suppressed weapons are available should they be needed. The author has also seen photographs of GIGN combat swimmers armed with Uzis. It is possible that the Uzi is in the GIGN armory for such ops because it would be less prone to malfunction after being carried underwater.

GIGN mental training includes analysis of previous GIGN operations and the psychology and methods of terrorist groups, especially those groups which GIGN is likely to go up against.

Being the HRU of one of the most technologically advanced countries in the world, GIGN, of course, has all sorts of high-tech hardware available for surveillance and detection. Everything from parabolic directional microphones to thermal imagers for locating targets within buildings is included. Pyrotechnics form an important part of the GIGN arsenal, which includes stun grenades, frame charges, and other specialized demolition devices.

Operationally, GIGN's record certainly justifies the expense and training lavished upon the unit. Since its formation, GIGN has rescued well over 250 hostages. Many of these rescues were in barricade situations within France since GIGN functions as the national SWAT team to deal with serious criminal hostage situations as well as with international terrorist incidents. GIGN's best-known operation was, however, against terrorists who had hijacked a school bus full of French school children in Djibouti during February 1976. In this operation (previously discussed), GIGN successfully rescued 29 of the 30 children due to its long-range shooting skill. Among the more well-known domestic hostage situations resolved by GIGN was the one at Clairvaux Prison in January 1978 when two inmates had taken a deputy warden and two guards hostage. Once again, GIGN resolved this situation with precision shooting. GIGN doesn't always have to resort to deadly force, though. In one interesting case, Capt. Prouteau ended a barricade situation by convincing the former paratrooper who had taken the hostages to surrender to Prouteau, a fellow paratrooper, in the name of the paratroop brotherhood.

GIGN has also been used to train Third World HRUs and thus increase France's prestige abroad. In 1979, for example, when radical Moslems occupied the Great Mosque at Mecca, it was GIGN which trained the Saudi National Guard prior to the operation to retake the mosque. Many of France's former colonies have also had their HRUs trained by GIGN. GIGN has reportedly also carried out some security assignments at French embassies in such troubled countries as Lebanon. It is known for a fact that when French diplomats were being held hostage at the French embassy in El Salvador, GIGN was moving into position to take out the terrorists when they surrendered. It is believed that some members of the left-wing press in France leaked GIGN's presence to the terrorists which caused them to surrender. If this is the case, GIGN's reputation was enough to end the crisis.

GIGN's use as a national SWAT team has helped keep the unit's skills sharp through frequent employment, as has exchange training with other Western HRUs. "Gigene" (as GIGN is often known in France) did suffer a setback to its reputation a couple of years ago for allegedly framing some members of the IRA, but the unit's skills remain at a high level and the GIGN ready team at Maisons-Alfort remains a formidable counter to terrorism. GIGN remains one of the world's "four-star" anti-terrorist units.

2nd REP

Additional anti-terrorist capability for certain types of rescues rests with the 2nd REP (Regiment Etranger De Parachutistes), which carried out a combat jump on 19 May 1978 to rescue white civilians at Kolwezi, Zaire. The 2nd REP would, however, only be used in large-scale rescue operations.

ROYAL DUTCH MARINES

Although certain members of the Dutch National Police are trained for anti-terrorist duties, the national HRU is composed of one company of the Royal Dutch Marines known as "Whiskey Company." With an authorized strength of 113 men, this company is divided into an HQ unit of 14 officers and men, including the unit

CO, a captain, and three 33-man platoons. One platoon is always ready 24 hours a day, while another is on standby status. The third platoon acts as a training unit and carries out a 16-week initial training program for recruits to the unit, after which they join an operational platoon for another 32 weeks of training as part of a five-man team.

Training includes the usual anti-terrorist specialties of rappelling, close combat—both hand-to-hand and with handguns and SMGs—entry techniques, and teamwork. Approximately 40 members of the company are trained as sharpshooters/countersnipers. Dutch Marine policy is to assign three snipers to each target to assure a kill if the "shoot" order is given. Snipers are armed with the FAL and the H&K G3SG/1. Normal assault weapons are the Uzi SMG backed up by the Colt Lawman Mark III .357 Magnum revolver. Normal technological hardware for surveillance and entry, pyrotechnics, and ballistic vests are available as well.

Many members of the unit are parachute trained and/or scuba trained. Cross-training is carried out with the SAS, GSG-9, and other Western anti-terrorist units. Because of the importance of Schipol Airport as an international air center, Whiskey Company does a lot of training there. Holland's many ports also necessitate extensive training in dealing with maritime hijackings, too. Interestingly enough, the unit receives extensive training in riot control in addition to the normal anti-terrorist training.

The Marine Close Combat Unit (as the HRU is also known) first saw operational use at Schevengingen jail in October 1974 during an insurrection led by a jailed Palestinian terrorist. The Marines assaulted at 3:40 A.M. when the prisoners' guard was down by throwing in stun grenades and then burning through the door's lock with a termic lance. As they rushed in, the Marines fired into the ceiling and subdued the prisoners in hand-to-hand combat. By most HRU standards, the Dutch have an overreluctance to take the life of an armed terrorist, and this operation was an example of that attitude. Fortunately, the mission was successful and there were no casualties. Since the prisoners were armed, however, they were certainly valid targets.

When South Moluccan terrorists seized a train in December 1975, the Marines were prepared to assault the train, but the seige ended without an assault being necessary. In May 1977, however, South Moluccans seized another train and a school, a seizure that ended weeks later with a successful assault on the train. (See Chapter 2.)

The unit was used again in March 1978 when South Moluccans seized a government building in Assen. When a hostage was shot, the Marines assaulted successfully, though six hostages were wounded.

These effective actions in the 1970s by the Royal Dutch Marines' HRU, combined with effective police intelligence measures, have done much to defuse the South Moluccans as a terrorist threat in Holland, but the Royal Dutch Marines HRU continues to train in case its special skills are called for in the future.

The BSB

Additional Dutch anti-terrorist capability exists in the "Brigade Speciale Beveiliginsopdrachten (BSB) of the "koncnklijke Marechaussee." This police anti-terrorist unit came into existence in 1975 and functions primarily in criminal situations where the Marines would not be called in, though it does handle certain hostage rescue situations.

ITALIAN HRUs

It can be confusing at times determining what Italy's primary national HRU is since there have been two rival units in existence; in fact, there was an additional ad-hoc unit which preceded both of them which makes the matter even more confusing.

GIS

It appears, however, that currently the GIS (Groupe Interventional Speciale) of the Carabinieri is the primary unit. This unit, consisting of 46 men primarily drawn from the parachute elements of the Carabinieri, is based near the town of Lavarno.

GIS members are trained rigorously to stay in top physical condition, running five kilometers and swimming two kilometers daily as well as practicing hand-to-hand combat. Their weapons training is also intensive, including their own version of the SAS "killing house" and scenarios with their executive officers acting as live "hostages" with targets placed nearby. Snipers are also well-trained and work on scenarios in conjunction with assault teams. Demolitions and breaching techniques, rappelling, and other entry methods are all rehearsed until the GIS can carry them out as a well-oiled machine. Training also takes place at Leonardo Di Vinci Airport in anti-hijacking techniques. Among other special training received by some members of GIS are alpini and incursori training. The latter is among the world's best combat swimmer training and should have prepared GIS swimmers should they have had to carry out an assault on the ship *Achille Lauro*.

The primary assault weapon for GIS is the H&K MP5 backed up by .357 Magnum revolvers.

NOCS

Italy's other HRU is the NOCS (Nucleo Operativo Centrale di Sicurezza), also known as "teste di cuoio" (leatherheads) because of the leather helmets they wear during assaults and training. (In contrast, GIS members normally wear ballistic helmets with face shields when assaulting, but no one seems to call them the "plastic heads"!) NOCS achieved fame for their rescue of kidnapped American General James Dozier from the Red Brigades.

Consisting of approximately 50 men, NOCS was created after the Aldo Moro kidnapping and trained at the Abbosanta Police Training Center on Sardinia. Like the GIS or other top HRUs, they receive constant physical training, including intensive instruction in judo and karate. Rappelling, high-speed driving, demolitions, and marksmanship are among the many other skills in which they receive training. NOCS also does a lot of night assault work using special optics on their Beretta M12 SMGs.

Like GSG-9, NOCS studies terrorist methods, including Red Brigade ideology and life-styles, until they can think like the terrorists. NOCS (and GIS, too) also receives sophisticated technological training in the use of electronic surveillance equipment.

In January 1982, members of NOCS became national heroes in Italy as they carried out a lightning raid on an apartment in Padua to free Gen. Dozier. Assaulting at just after 11:30 A.M. to take advantage of the bustle on the streets and the noise of a construction crew's bulldozer nearby, ten NOCS men arrived in front of the apartment building in a moving van and were dressed in civilian clothes (though they wore ballistic vests and balaclavas). One assault team member split off to seal a supermarket door near the apartment entrance so the innocent bystanders could not wander out, while the other nine men assaulted the apartment. One member of NOCS—a competitive weightlifter—took out the door quickly; another NOCS man efficiently took out a terrorist encountered in the hall with a karate blow to the forehead. As still another terrorist prepared to execute Gen. Dozier, a NOCS man felled him with a blow from the butt of his M12.

The primary assault arm of NOCS is the Beretta M12 SMG backed up by the Beretta 92 pistol. Since the NOCS trains heavily for night assaults, night optics are available for its M12s and sniper's rifles. The usual gamut of technological aids, such as stun grenades, are available to both GIS and NOCS. NOCS seems to have fallen into disfavor, however, due to the actions of some of its members who reportedly tortured Red Brigade suspects.

Both the Italian Army and Navy also reportedly have anti-terrorist units. It can be assumed that the latter unit is drawn from the Incursori, who are among the world's best combat swimmers.

SPANISH GEO AND UEI

Spanish anti-terrorist forces have an especially difficult task since they must counter threats from the left, such as GRAPO and ETA, as well as threats from the right. As a result the men selected for GEO, Grupo Especial de Operaciones, the national HRU of the Policia Nacional, must be apolitical.

GEO, formed in 1978, came into existence later than many of the other European anti-terrorist units but it has proven to be a highly effective anti-terrorist force. When forming the unit, its first commander, Garcia Quijada, had 400 applicants from which he selected 70. During the selection process, this number was further trimmed to 58 men. Selection was geared toward singling out men with physical strength, intelligence, dedication, self-control, and excellent reflexes.

Once selected for GEO, training consisted of physical training, including distance running, martial arts, swimming, skiing, climbing, parachuting, and scuba; demolitions; topography/land navigation; photography; high-speed driving; psychology; building assault techniques; marksmanship; languages; rappelling from buildings, helicopters, etc.; and terrorist organization and techniques. Even after becoming a full-fledged member of GEO, one can expect to train 12 hours per day, with many night exercises included.

Currently, GEO has a strength of about 120 men which is divided into 24 five-man teams. Although each man is trained in various techniques, he also is a specialist on the team in one of the five areas of expertise—

small arms, demolitions, communications, combat swimming, or sniping. At least one team is always ready for instant deployment around the clock.

GEO members can be identified by their brown berets and, when operational, their special combat vests in which they carry a handgun, knife, radio, light, rappelling equipment, gas mask, grenades, etc. Despite the strong domestic arms industry, GEO is primarily equipped with German weapons, at least partially as a result of GSG-9's help in setting up the unit. GEO handguns are either the H&K P9S or the Manurhin MR-73. The principal assault weapon is the H&K MP5 with the MP-5K available for special use. The MP5SD with special night optics is also available. The two sniper's rifles are the Mauser 66T and the H&K G-3SG/1.

GEO has carried out some very important operations which remain virtually unknown. It has also received a certain amount of publicity for certain successful operations, especially the handling of the Central Bank of Barcelona siege in May 1981. Twenty-four right-wing terrorists had occupied the Central Bank and taken more than 200 hostages.

GEO was called in, and approximately 60 men of the unit were flown to Barcelona and deployed around the bank. While GEO snipers took up shooting positions, demolition experts moved through the sewers under the bank to check the possibility of blasting in from below. When given the order to go in, GEO assaulted with MP5s and, despite the large number of terrorists and hostages, completed the rescue with only a single hostage wounded. One terrorist was killed and ten captured, though the remainder managed to slip away amidst the large number of hostages.

GEO was also deployed to rescue singer Julio Iglesias's father from kidnappers and to free hostages at the Bank of Bilbao. Though not as well known as the SAS, GSG-9, or GIGN, GEO is a first-rate anti-terrorist unit, of which the citizens of Spain can feel proud.

Guardia Civil

There is additional anti-terrorist capability within the Guardia Civil. These include the UEI (Unidad Especial de Intervencion) and the GAR (Grupos Antiterroristas Rurales). Although GEO is the best known of Spain's anti-terrorist units, many experts within Spain and elsewhere consider UEI superior to GEO. The Guardia Civil, a militarized national police force with special responsibility for the rural areas, comes under the control of the ministries of interior and defense. Formed in 1978 with assistance from GIGN, UEI has country-wide responsibility. Its primary missions involve hostage rescue, suppression of kidnappings and rescuing of victims, aircraft or other hijackings, prison riots, hunting down dangerous escaped convicts, and carrying out VIP protection in high-threat situations.

UEI's selection process is very rigid, as only 2 percent of the applicants actually make it into the unit. Once selected, a member will be assigned to the administrative team, one of the eight assault teams, or the specialized negotiations, communications, intelligence, or technical units.

Training includes most of the HRU skills enumerated for other units. Much stress is placed on physical fitness, especially agility and ability in the martial arts. Swimming skills, including scuba, are also important since Spain has so many ports. Rappelling and climbing skills both on building and natural heights are stressed, the latter more than in some HRUs because UEI works in many mountainous areas. Training in assault tactics receives special attention with various types of day and night scenarios being set up. Breaching and entry techniques with and without explosives are combined with other training to lend as much realism as possible. UEI's inventory includes sophisticated low-light optics and listening or other surveillance devices, which members of the unit learn to use with great skill.

UEI members are trained for versatility, and training

scenarios are geared to keeping them sharp between operations. Scenarios duplicate hostage or barricade situations involving airports, airliners, trains, ships, docks, prisons, embassies, and other installations. It should be noted that UEI would normally be the unit which would respond to a hijacking of an aircraft, ship, or train.

Shooting training also emphasizes scenarios and realism in an attempt to train the operative to be cool under pressure and to fire in connection with an entry. Using mannequins as targets, scenarios are created in which it is necessary to eliminate "terrorists" without hitting hostages nearby. In one scenario, for example, two terrorist targets will be positioned on each side of a hostage target in a vehicle, and UEI snipers must take out the terrorists with head shots at 150 meters without touching the hostage target. Other scenarios use live "hostages" positioned near terrorist targets. These include scenarios which require gaining entry and then rapid shooting to score double taps on the "terrorists'" heads with the SMG or handgun and long-range head shots at 120 to 200 meters with nearby live "hostages."

To build a steady hand on the part of the shooters and poise under fire on the part of the "target," the GIGN technique of scoring hits on a small ceramic plate worn on the front of a ballistic vest by a fellow unit member is practiced with the handgun at 20 meters. Another GIGN technique practiced by UEI is shooting while rappelling down buildings or from helicopters.

UEI is armed with either large-magazine capacity 9mm autos, probably the Astra or Star, or .357 Magnum revolvers, probably the Astra or Llama. The principal assault weapon is the H&K MP5 in various forms, including the MP5A2, MP5A3, MP5K, and MP5SD. U.S.-made 12-gauge fighting shotguns are used. The primary sniper's rifle is the Mauser 66SP; 5.56mm and 7.62mm self-loading rifles are also available, as are light and medium machine guns, CS gas guns, and other special-purpose arms. Additional equipment includes ballistic helmets (though UEI often assaults in black balaclavas); ballistic vests; high-tech listening and surveillance equipment; various types of radios; scaling ladders and other special-purpose entry equipment; and stun grenades and other explosives.

Among UEI's successful deployments have been hostage rescues at prisons, rescue of a kidnapee from ETA terrorists, the capture of a large number of ETA terrorists, seizure of ETA weapons and explosives, countering of ship and aircraft hijackings, VIP protection assignments, foreign embassy security details, the killing of four GRAPO terrorists during a shootout, and various other hostage situations. It should be noted that when carrying out the embassy security duties, UEI members often posed as members of the embassy staffs in order to remain low-profile.

UEI has carried out at least one overseas advisory mission to Ecuador. Like GEO, UEI is a very well-trained, very professional HRU, which acts as an important counterweight to the terrorists who have been a threat to Spanish democracy.

BELGIAN ESI

Belgium's national anti-terrorist unit—ESI (Escadron Special d'Intervention)—like France's HRU—is drawn from the national militarized police, the Gendarmerie Royale. Though ESI is the official name, the unit is often known by its codename "Diana." The Gendarmerie normally falls under the Ministry of Defense but in certain situations may come under control of the Ministry of Justice or Interior. The Gendarmerie is actually considered one of the armed forces. ESI is not only called upon in hostage situations but also those involving terrorist bombs, though EOD is actually carried out by the SEDEE (Service d'Enlevement et de Destruction des Engins Explosifs).

The approximately 200 members of ESI tend to be quite young, usually in their early twenties, and extremely physically fit. Physical training includes martial arts, climbing, rappelling, and swimming. Shooting is, of course, stressed, with the ability to identify and neutralize targets quickly in a tactical situation being preeminent. Some members of ESI receive additional shooting training on their own initiative through BLEA. Many ESI members receive training as parachutists, commandos, combat swimmers, or mountain specialists. Cross-training with GIGN, GSG-9, or other Western anti-terrorist units also takes place.

Use of specialized equipment, including stun grenades, surveillance equipment, and demolitions for forcing an entry, is stressed in training, which also includes terrorist theory and methods. Like GIGN, ESI also functions as a national SWAT team, and attention is therefore given to criminal activities which might require action by ESI. The unit has, for example, been involved in stake-outs in an attempt to counter the large number of murders at supermarkets which have taken place in Belgium at the hands of a group known as the "crazies."

ESI is armed with the Browning Hi-Power as their sidearm and the H&K MP5 as the primary assault weapon. H&K MP5SDs are also available with various types of special optics. ESI is also equipped with Remington 870 12-gauge fighting shotguns for certain forced entry or roadblock situations. Snipers, who receive intensive training, are armed with the Steyr SSG or the FN. Tear gas guns, ballistic vests, and gas masks are available as needed.

ESI is backed up by the GRT (Grupe de Repression du Terrorisme) of the Judiciary Police, a plainclothes, anti-terrorist intelligence-gathering unit which coordinates all anti-terrorist activities. The Judiciary Police, it should be noted, are roughly equivalent to the FBI. In certain extreme situations outside of Belgium, elements of the Belgian Para-Commando Regiment might be used, though they receive little or no special training in the rescue of hostages in a barricade situation. Members of the Para-Commandos, especially the ESR (Equipes Speciales de Recherche) have been involved, though, along with ESI in supermarket stake-outs to counter the "crazies." All of the author's sources in Belgium, however, indicate that it is very unlikely that ESI, though the national HRU, would ever be employed outside Belgium.

SWEDEN

Sweden has often had a tendency to think of terrorism as a problem which affects other nations but not Sweden. It has, in fact, often served as a haven for other countries' dissidents. The assassination of Olof Palme, however, has brought home the fact that Sweden is not immune to the violence affecting other countries. During the 1970s some embassies in Sweden were also occupied by terrorists. As a result, Sweden has had an anti-terrorist capability since the early Seventies, though normally the unit has stayed low profile.

This unit is actually part of the Stockholm police, but it acts as a national HRU as well. If deployed outside Stockholm, it comes under the command of the Rikspolis (the State police). This unit has a strength of 200 men, which includes the Swedish riot police. The force is divided into 40-man platoons, but the basic operating unit is the ten-man team, four per platoon. One small subunit of 15 men exists in Gothenburg.

This Swedish unit has received training from the SAS, GSG-9, and the Israeli GHQ unit. Normal HRU skills (i.e., shooting, assault tactics, rappelling, use of pyrotechnics) and riot control have been taught. This author is not aware of any concerted effort to train members of the unit as parachutists or combat swimmers, but the large maritime industry in Sweden would seem to indicate that at least some members of the unit be scuba and small-boat trained.

Armament consists of the Walther PP 7.65mm pistol, the M45 SMG (the Swedish K), the AK4 rifle (a modified G3), and possibly the M41 sniper's rifle.

NORWAY

Norway's national HRU is the Beredskapstrop (readiness troop) of the National Police. Created in 1975, this 50-man unit is quite competent and is based at Oslo. There are between four and twelve members in the basic operational unit, which is broken down even further into two-man teams. These two-man teams always work together as partners for normal police work and on the "buddy system" for HRU work. When the unit goes operational in a hostage situation, it comes directly under the Minister of Justice. Hijackings at Gardermoen Airport would be handled by this unit.

Basic training course for the unit runs three weeks and stresses combat shooting, assault tactics, rappelling, etc. Training continues for two to three days a week to keep skills sharp as long as the men are assigned to the unit. The members of this unit have reportedly received parachute training at Trandum. All are also trained to operate from helicopters and presumably at least some are trained in scuba techniques. The principal assault weapon is the H&K MP5 SMG backed up by a S&W .357 Magnum revolver or a 9mm auto. The unit is also equipped with sniper's rifles, but the author is not aware of which one.

Backing up the Beredskapstrop is a military anti-terrorist platoon of 40 men formed in 1984. This unit is based at the Norwegian airborne/ranger school at Trandum and is trained in airborne, ranger, scuba, etc. Some are HALO qualified. All members of the unit are army volunteers who serve in the unit for at least three years. Training has been carried out with the SAS, SBS, and GSG-9; the training with the SBS presumably included special attention to protection of North Sea oil rigs since the SBS has this mission in the United Kingdom. Among weapons in use with the unit are the Sterling L2A3 SMG and the Norwegian version of the FAL.

FINLAND

Finland's national HRU is the Osasto Karhu ("Bear Unit") of the Helsinki Mobile Police Department. This 40-man unit was created in 1977 and had its genesis in an EOD unit formed in 1974. This unit works directly under the Ministry of the Interior and has responsibility for hostage or other terrorist situations throughout the country.

GSG-9 and the Swedish HRU have helped train the Finns. There have also been exchanges of information with HRUs from the United States, Austria, Holland, Norway, Britain, and France. Members of the unit are selected from veteran police officers and given training in combat shooting, assault tactics, terrorist psychology, negotiations, use of pyrotechnics and demolitions, rappelling, and other skills. It is not known if the unit still retains any EOD responsibility. Helsinki-Vantaa Airport does fall within its responsibilities, however, should a hijacking occur there.

Armament includes the S&W .357 Magnum revolver, H&K MP5, Uzi, and Suomi SMGs. SAKO shotguns are available for special situations. The unit is also equipped with sniper's rifles.

DENMARK

Interestingly enough, the best of the Danish anti-terrorist units is the one drawn from the Fromandskorpset (the Royal Danish Navy Combat Swimmers). This unit primarily has anti-terrorist responsibility for ports, oil rigs, and ships, but in certain situations it might be deployed for other HRU functions. Based at Kongsore Torpedo Station, the unit consists of 40 to 50 men who have received extensive special ops training and are parachute, ranger, scuba qualified. Additional training in combat shooting, assault tactics, infiltration tactics, and other skills has been received to complement the unit's already extensive skills. The unit has trained with the SBS, U.S. SEALs and U.S. Special Forces, GSG-9, GIGN, and others.

The principal assault weapon is the Swedish K SMG, but G3 rifles and the MG-62 MG are also used. Snipers are normally drawn from the Danish Army and are assigned for anti-terrorist situations. Reportedly, the Danish Army is also developing an Army HRU, probably drawn from the Jaegerkorpset (the Danish Rangers).

PET

There is also a police anti-terrorist unit known as PET (Politiets Efterretningstjeneste) drawn from the State Police Intelligence Service. The Unit is dispersed around the country but is called together periodically for training or when needed for an operation. The unit has received training from GSG-9 and the SAS. It is unclear whose responsibility a hijacking at Kastrup Airport would be, but presumably it would fall to PET. The author does not have much information about armament, but the unit reportedly assaults with 9mm SGMs, probably the MP5 or Swedish K.

PORTUGUESE GRUPO DE OPERACOES ESPECIAIS

Portugal's national HRU is the Grupo de Operacoes Especiais (the Special Operations Group) of the Policia de Seguranca Publica. The unit was first begun in 1979, but it did not officially come into existence as the national HRU until 1982. Based near Lisbon, this unit has received help in training from the SAS and is organized and trained along SAS lines. Members of the unit are volunteers from the police but also include many former members of the Portuguese Commandos, presumably who later joined the police.

The unit receives extensive shooting training in a

well-designed shooting house similar to that of the SAS. The usual gamut of additional anti-terrorist skills, including hand-to-hand combat, rappelling, and use of pyrotechnics and demolitions, are taught, but this unit also places great stress on negotiating and has very well-trained negotiators assigned. Originally, the unit was not parachute qualified but it is likely that some or all members have received parachute training within the last year or so.

The unit wears a dark blue SWAT-style utility uniform when operational, with a gas mask, ski mask/balaclava, and Bristol ballistic vest. One obvious SAS influence is the low-slung SAS-type holster in which the Browning Hi-Power is carried. Also like the SAS, the principal assault weapon is the H&K MP5. For sniping, reportedly the PSG-1 and Walther WA2000 rifle are used.

The only operation for which the unit is known to have been called out occurred in 1983 when the Turkish Embassy in Portugal was occupied; however, the terrorists had blown themselves up by the time the unit arrived. The combination of SAS training and the "stiffening" provided by the former commandos should make this unit a reasonably capable one.

SWITZERLAND

In 1978 Switzerland tried to found a national HRU, but the motion was defeated in Parliament; therefore, canton or city police handle the HRU duties for their respective areas. Just as the Swiss reserve military system works well, this system of local HRUs seems to work relatively well in Switzerland. Bern and Zurich have especially capable units designated the "Stern" unit and the "Enzian" unit. These units tend to average about 50 men, and their duties also include VIP protection and airport security, along with HRU. Once again, skills include many of those associated with HRUs but not normally parachuting. A few members, possibly those from the Lake Police, are, however, scuba trained. Assault tactics, hand-to-hand, and marksmanship are emphasized. GSG-9 has also helped train most of these canton HRUs. Generally, the Zurich unit is considered to be the premier unit.

Armament varies from unit to unit, but the SIG-Saur P6 (a.k.a. P225) and SIG-Sauer P-226 are known to be used as sidearms. The most popular assault weapon is the ubiquitous H&K MP5, with MP5SDs available for special situations. Some units are known to be equipped with H&K33 5.56mm rifles, but some units have snipers armed with the Steyr SSG 7.62mm sniper's rifle, too. Shotguns are also available if needed, as are ballistic vests, stun grenades, and other pyrotechnics or technological equipment.

Swiss HRUs have seen operational employment on more than one occasion. When terrorists occupied the Polish Embassy in Bern, for example, 20 members of the Bern Police HRU carried out a successful assault using CS gas and stun grenades and rescued 14 hostages and arrested four terrorists. In March 1984, the Geneva HRU sent in men posing as caterers to rescue 62 hostages aboard a hijacked Air France 737.

Members of some canton's police forces, often from the HRUs, are detached from their departments, given intensive training, and serve as sky marshals aboard Swissair flights. Armament is the P225 with special lighter loads and expanding bullets. Upon returning to their units, these men are far more qualified to deal with an aircraft hijacking based on their knowledge of procedures at airports and aboard the aircraft.

IRELAND

To handle hostage incidents, the Irish Republic relies on the Special Branch of the National Police (Garda Siochana). The HRU was originally formed in 1978 and formally became the national HRU in 1980. Its strength appears to be about 40 men who have received training from the RCMP (Royal Canadian Mounted Police), GSG-9, and other Western anti-terrorist units. Training includes the normal HRU skills, though parachute or scuba training are apparently not included; it is possible, however, that at least one or two members of the unit has some skill in the latter. The HRU assaults with the Uzi 9mm SMG backed up by a Walther 9mm auto pistol. Sniper's rifles reportedly are the Remington 700.

To back up the Special Branch HRU in an extreme situation, Ireland has a small Special Ranger unit as part of the Army. Based at Curragh Military Camp, this unit consists of about 70 men and has had some special assault training from the Royal Dutch Marines and some U.S. units (though whether Delta, Special Forces, or Rangers is not known to the author).

AUSTRIAN COBRA UNIT

Austria's primary special unit is the Gendarmeriee-insatzkommando (Gendarmarie Special Unit), but it is normally known as the Cobra Unit. In addition to functioning as the national HRU, this unit also does certain special security duties (i.e., at OPEC Head-quarters and airports) and occasionally provides VIP protective services. Unit strength is about 200 men who have received training in combat shooting, hand-to-hand combat, riot control, building assault tactics, rappelling, and other special skills expected of an HRU. GSG-9, GIGN, and the Israeli GHQ units have all helped with Cobra's training. In addition to anti-terrorist duties, Cobra performs certain anti-criminal duties with dangerous criminals much as GIGN, ESI, or some other national police HRUs do.

The primary handgun for Cobra has been the Browning Hi-Power, though there are some indications that the Manurhin .357 Mag may be adopted. Although the primary assault SMG seems to be the Uzi, Cobra is also armed with the AM-180 in .22 long rifle caliber. The

Steyr AUG assault rifle in 5.56mm is also used. In the sniper/countersniper role, the Steyr SSG 7.62mm is used with various types of optics, including sophisticated night ones, depending on the situation. Ballistic vests, stun grenades, CS gas, and other special-purpose equipment and armament are available if needed.

GREEK DEA

The Dimoria Eidikon Apostolon (Special Mission Platoon) of the Athens City Police is a SWAT unit trained to act as an HRU. This unit was established in the mid-1970s and is composed of about 50 men. They have trained primarily in Greece but have had training assistance from GSG-9, the SAS, the Royal Dutch Marines, and other top HRUs. They have also trained with such Greek elite units as the Army special forces and the Alpine Raiding Company. Armament consists of S&W .38 Special revolvers, H&K MP5, and Uzi SMGs, and, reportedly, Bren LMGs. There do not appear to be any snipers in the unit.

There are also two special anti-hijacking units stationed at the airports in Athens and Thessaloniki. These units are part of the city police force but have received HRU training, including assault tactics on airliners. They were formed in 1980 and are armed with the same revolver and SMGs as the DEA. From the poor record of security at Athens's Hellinikon Airport, these units obviously could use some improvement.

TURKISH OIKB

Because of the various terrorist threats faced by Turkey, including the TPLA (Turkish People's Liberation Army) and various Armenian groups, the necessity for an anti-terrorist capability is obvious. Unfortunately, rather than a few well-trained men to act as a national HRU, Turkey has formed 12 regional companies of the Ozel Intihar Kommando Bolugu (The Jandara Suicide

Commandos) to handle anti-terrorist duties. Theoretically 150 men strong, only three of these companies actually appear to exist, and they are stationed at Ankara, Izmir, and Istanbul. The one at Istanbul would appear to have responsibility for incidents at Yesilkov Airport.

The existing OIKB companies are reasonably well-trained, having received special forces, airmobile, rappelling, and riot control training as well as weapons use and hand-to-hand. Turkish toughness is, of course, legendary. The OIKB's principal assault arm is the H&K MP5 with the Colt .45 auto as the principal sidearm. H&K33 5.56mm rifles are in the armory.

The unit saw operational usage in October 1980 during the rescue of hostages in an aircraft hijacking, and reportedly assaulted with .45 autos.

There are also elements of the Turkish National Police which function as HRUs, but they are really more akin to U.S. SWAT teams. These units are normally armed with S&W .38 Special revolvers or Browning Hi-Powers, H&K MP5s, and .308 caliber sniper's rifles, probably the H&K G3SG/1. These units receive a lot of training in riot control and internal security as well as HRU tactics.

EASTERN EUROPE

Since the Soviet Union has many ties with terrorists, there have not been many "terrorist" incidents committed against the Soviet Union and its allies. There have, however, been hijackings of airliners, especially East German and Polish ones at various times. It is, therefore, almost certain that the Soviet Union maintains certain troops trained to retake an airliner or to rescue a high-ranking party member taken hostage. The Spetsnaz, the special operations troops of the Soviet Army, may have certain troops trained for hostage rescue or other anti-hijacking operations. The author feels, however, that it is also likely that such units exist within the MVD

(Ministry of Internal Security) or the Kremlin Guard Unit of the KGB. The latter particularly would be likely to have some men trained for a rescue operation.

The only unit within the Warsaw Pact known to the author to be designated an anti-terrorist unit is a special element of the 4101st Polish Paratroop Battalion, which was deployed in 1984 during the trial of four police officers being tried for murdering activist priest Father Jerzy Popieluszko. It is also possible that members of the Batalion Ochrony Rzadu, which is a special guard unit for Polish Communist officials, has had some HRU training. Among other Warsaw Pact countries, East Germany's Felix Dzerzhinsky Wach Regiment der MfS is probably the most likely to have members trained for the HRU role.

CHAPTER 5

U.S. Anti-Terrorist Capability

The U.S. lagged behind many other countries in establishing an anti-terrorist capability. Although an interim anti-terrorist unit known as "Blue Light" composed of about 40 men drawn primarily from the 5th Special Forces Group (Airborne) was initially assigned the anti-terrorist mission, this unit was always considered only a stopgap unit to fill in until Special Forces Operational Detachment-Delta became fully operational.

DELTA

Delta, which was activated in November 1977, was primarily the brainchild of a Special Forces officer named Charles Beckwith, who had served with the SAS during the 1960s. Beckwith felt the U.S. needed a unit capable of carrying out deep penetration raids, intelligence gathering, POW rescues, and other SAS-style missions and had been pushing for such a unit for many years. It was not until after the GSG-9 rescue at Mogadishu made world headlines and prompted the Executive Branch of the U.S. Government to ask the Joint

Chiefs of Staff about U.S. anti-terrorist capabilities, however, that Beckwith was given the go-ahead to form Delta.

Delta originally had only a small cadre assigned since Beckwith wanted to run a selection course along SAS lines to choose his men. Even before volunteers could undergo this selection course, though, they had to pass a tough physical test which included 37 sit-ups in under a minute, 33 push-ups in under a minute, a two-mile run in under 16 1/2 minutes, a 100-meter swim (while fully dressed, including jump boots), and two other events. Prior to the actual selection course, prospective Delta members also had to do an 18-mile speed march. Finally, those who had made it through the preliminary stages took part in the selection course, the first of which was run in the Uwharrie National Forest in North Carolina. This selection course was patterned very much after the SAS Brecon Beacons course which tests physical endurance and individual initiative and tenacity. Upon successfully completing the selection course, potential members of Delta underwent psychological evaluation and interviews, the latter of which included questions about special skills such as driving tanks, picking locks, or piloting aircraft. Of the 30 men who took part in the first selection course, seven were kept for Delta.

Although Delta drew heavily from the Special Forces, men from all other branches of the Army were eligible as well. Most of those in the second selection course, though, were from the 10th Special Forces Group (Airborne). This course was run at Camp Dawson in West Virginia because it more closely resembled the Brecon Beacons. Five out of 60 made it into Delta from this group.

By the third course, quite a few Rangers as well as a substantial number of Special Forces troopers were trying out, but still only 14 out of 70 made it into Delta.

The selection process continued until May 1978, at which time there were 73 men who had made it through the course in addition to the original cadre. These men were put through a 19-week "operator's" course in which they learned the basic skills of the anti-terrorist "commando"—combat shooting, communications, assault tactics, breaching techniques, first aid, managing hostages, use of high-tech optics, high-speed and specialized driving, land navigation, explosive ordnance recce and disposal, hand-to-hand combat, airmobile and airborne insertions, rappelling, and small boat insertions. Rappelling included extensive work on buildings as well as fast roping and other techniques from choppers. Evacuation of hostages via rappelling was also practiced. Free-climbing techniques were learned on buildings and rock faces. Anyone not already parachute-qualified upon being selected for Delta was sent to jump school.

Organization was along SAS lines as well, using squadrons which were broken into troops. Initially, Delta consisted of one operational squadron, but a second was added as enough men became available. Training in various esoteric skills, of course, continued as long as a man stayed with Delta, and members of the unit were constantly pursuing some type of useful and specialized training which would increase their effectiveness.

Shooting took up a large amount of training time—three to four hours daily, five days per week, in fact. At their own sophisticated version of the SAS "Killing House," Delta created the "House of Horrors," which had four rooms. The first room had pop-up friend-or-foe targets and was used as a "warm-up" room. The second room had entry and immediate engagement scenarios set up. The third was designed for night shooting and breaching. The fourth was a mockup of an aircraft cabin. Assaults were often practiced in four- or six-man teams. The four-man assault team usually handled entries into a single room and used handguns, though the "tailgunner" might be armed with a shotgun. The six-man team practiced assaults on multiple rooms and was normally armed with SMGs.

The standards set for Delta's snipers were very high. At 600 yards they were expected to score 100 out of 100, while at 1,000 yards 90 out of 100 was the minimum. Legendary Special Forces officer "Bull" Simons, who had led the Son Tay Raid in North Vietnam, helped Delta snipers develop special loads for their rifles. Targets for the snipers and in the "House of Horrors" were often photos of known terrorists. Based upon Simons' tutelage, Delta snipers loaded their own ammunition.

Since aircraft hijacking was foreseen as a primary threat to be countered by Delta, the FAA (Federal Aviation Administration) provided the unit with a 727 for training in assault tactics. Many training exercises were also run at Kennedy Airport and other large U.S. airports. Members of Delta studied all aspects of aircraft and airport operations so that they could plan assaults based on various contingencies. All types of airliners were studied, with special emphasis on blind spots for an approach prior to an assault, location of hatches, visible warning lights on the control panel in the cockpit if a hatch were opened, and hundreds of other details which could be critical during an operation.

About eight months after its formation, Delta proved so impressive in demonstrations for high-ranking officers that it was considered "on-line" ahead of schedule, and "Blue Light" was phased out. Intelligence on terrorists and terrorist acts was fed directly to Delta by the CIA, FBI, NSA, etc. Delta also had its own sophisticated communications equipment, including a man-portable satellite link.

Delta's armament was fairly traditional U.S. military at the beginning. The handgun was a U.S. Government Model .45 auto which had received extensive accurizing by Delta's own gunsmiths. Each .45, in fact, came with various sets of springs to allow for different loads. Some Browning Hi-Powers, S&W .357 Magnums, H&K P7s, Walther PPKs, and silenced High Standard and Ruger .22 autos were also available for special use. Delta originally used the .45 M3A1 "Greasegun" with a special selector switch as its SMG, but later MP5s and Uzis saw usage. On Grenada, for example, Delta reportedly used suppressed versions of the Uzi. The CAR-15 version of the M-16 has also been used. The Remington 40XB has been the primary sniper's rifle. For the Iranian Mission, the H&K 21 machine gun and M79 and M203 40mm grenade launchers were included in the armament to lend additional firepower. In certain situations Delta operators also use the M60 GPMG. Delta is now reportedly using the Sidewinder (and perhaps the Benelli Police/Military) fighting shotgun for certain assault or security situations.

The usual array of ballistic vests, night-vision devices, surveillance equipment, and special-purpose pyrotechnics/demolitions is available to Delta as is CS gas.

Delta members were allowed to visit European and other foreign cities to recce possible terrorist targets and to get used to operating in strange milieus. In the summer of 1979, three members of Delta traveled to Puerto Rico to work with the FBI unit assigned the HRU task at the Pan American Games. Foreign travel also included exchange training with the SAS, GSG-9, GIGN, the Israelis, and others. Ties with these units were so close, in fact, that GSG-9's Ulrich Wegener and GIGN's Christian Prouteau, along with members of the SAS and some other anti-terrorist units, observed a Delta exercise in the fall of 1979 just before the U.S. embassy in Teheran was occupied.

Once the U.S. embassy was seized on 5 November, Delta went on alert for possible use in a rescue mission. Most of the unit was moved to a secure training site away from the stockade at Fort Bragg, North Carolina, where Delta was normally based. Delta intelligence specialists also started compiling intelligence about the embassy, hostages, Iranian armed forces, and other factors in preparation for planning a rescue. Satellite photos, and TV and film people who had been in Iran, as well as other sources, were tapped for intelligence.

Later in the planning GSG-9 even offered to help get
Delta operators into Teheran as news cameramen.

As plans began to evolve, Delta snipers started training as light-machine gunners with the H&K Model 21.
Other members of the unit worked on mastering the
M203 and M79 40mm grenade launchers. Because of the
nine-foot walls around the embassy, scaling techniques
were reviewed and drilled endlessly. The use of explosives to open doors and punch holes in the walls was
explored and rehearsed. Intensive night training was
undertaken as well since it was likely any assault would
be mounted in darkness.

As the assault plan evolved, various insertion methods
were considered—by truck from the Turkish border, by
parachute, by helicopters. Finally, the decision was
made to go with the helicopters.

As intelligence poured in, it was learned that three
hostages were held outside the embassy compound at
the Iranian Foreign Ministry. To handle this assault, a
special 13-man team drawn from Special Forces Detachment Europe began training in Germany.

More and more personnel became involved since a
company of Rangers was deemed necessary to seize and
secure Manzariyeh Airfield to which the hostages would
be ferried from Teheran for evacuation aboard a C-141.
Two other sites were also selected—Desert One, where
Delta and ground team members including Farsi-
speaking drivers, Iranian translators, Delta members,
and the team from Germany would land and meet the
helicopters, and Desert Two, where the assault force
and its drivers would spend the day of the assault while
they awaited darkness. Beckwith originally had intended
for 72 members of Delta to be involved, but this number would increase to 93.

Delta was broken into three groups. *Blue Group*
was comprised of 40 men who would assault the resi-
dence of the DCM (Deputy Chief of Mission), the
ambassador's quarters, chancellery, and other buildings
in that part of the compound to free the hostages held

there. *Red Group*, also comprised of 40 men, would assault the commissary and staff cottages to free any hostages in that part of the compound. *White Element*, consisting of 13 men, was assigned the mission of securing Roosevelt Avenue to prevent reinforcements from arriving and of seizing and holding a nearby soccer stadium to be used as an emergency helicopter landing zone (LZ).

Delta's plan was to hit hard and take out every Iranian guard that was encountered. With its H&K 21s, the White Element would interdict reinforcement routes, while the Blue and Red Groups and the team from Special Forces Detachment Europe carried out their assaults and freed the hostages. The hostages would then be hustled aboard choppers and evacuated while members of Delta provided security and then rolled up their perimeter and were lifted out themselves. The plan called for Delta to enter Iran on the night of 24 April, lie up during the day of 25 April, carry out the assault on the night of 25 April, and fly out of Iran with the hostages early on the morning of 26 April.

Obviously, the two greatest problems with the plan were getting Delta into and out of Teheran and the fact that such a large complex would have to be assaulted and cleared since the exact location of the hostages was not known. In December 1979, the CIA got an agent into Iran to find answers to some of the questions Delta's intelligence specialists had to have answered. The key effort was to figure out where in the embassy compound the hostages were being held.

During the first months of 1980, training intensified. Marine pilots chosen to fly the choppers, Delta, Air Force special ops pilots, and Rangers carried out rehearsals in Arizona. During February and March, full-scale rehearsals were run including the various elements involved. During the months of training, more than 100 assaults were carried out by Delta on mockups of the embassy. Throughout this training, U.S. intelligence agencies began to narrow the possible location of the hostages within the embassy compound until shortly before the mission was launched. At that time it was learned that all hostages in the embassy compound were held in the chancellery. Finally, on 16 April, President Carter gave the go-ahead for the mission code-named "Eagle Claw."

Six C-130s from the 8th Special Operations Squadron flew the men, equipment, and fuel from Egypt to Desert One, 265 miles from Teheran, on the night of 24 April. Eight RH-53D "Sea Stallion" helicopters were launched from the *U.S.S. Nimitz* in the Arabian Sea to rendezvous at Desert One. The plan called for these choppers, which included two extras to allow for problems, to fly the raiding party to Desert Two 50 miles from Teheran. They would be met there by agents already in Iran with trucks and vans which would be used to drive them into Teheran where the assault on the embassy compound would be launched at 2300 on 25 April. To suppress Iranian mobs, military reinforcements, or aircraft, two AC-130 "Spectre" gunships would be available to lay down a hail of 20mm and 40mm fire. Eighty Rangers would be airlifted from Egypt to secure the airstrip at Manzariyeh, 35 miles from Teheran, where the C-141s would fly the hostages and raiding party out of Iran. Originally, an air strike on Iranian oil facilities was planned in conjunction with the raid, but President Carter cancelled the mission shortly before the raid was launched.

The first C-130 to land at Desert One carried Col. Beckwith, some of his Delta operatives, and an Air Force Combat Control Team to guide in the remaining aircraft. The other aircraft carrying the remainder of Delta, equipment, and fuel for the choppers arrived safely as well, but the problems with the helicopters, which had encountered a sandstorm, delayed their arrival at Desert One. By the time the choppers did arrive, two had to be scratched due to mechanical problems, leaving the bare minimum to carry out the operation successfully based on all estimates. When one of the remaining six choppers developed mechanical problems, Col. Beckwith was reluctantly forced to abort the mission. Unfortunately, during the evacuation of the raiding force and the aircrew, one chopper crashed into a C-130 loaded with ammo and fuel, thereby causing fires and explosions. The result: the death of eight men and injury to several others.

Some criticisms of the raid, though not of Delta's performance, can be offered. The fact that only eight choppers were taken rather than nine or ten is one possible criticism, especially since normal special ops doctrine calls for 100 percent redundancy. Politics may have played some part, too, since U.S. Air Force special ops or pararescue pilots might have been more suited to such a mission than the Marine Corps pilots that were chosen. Most of all, though, the ad hoc assembling of assets for the Iranian mission illustrated that Delta could not operate in a vacuum. It should be noted, too, that reportedly Delta had forces in place in Iran for a possible rescue on two or more occasions prior to the abortive raid, but in both cases the mission was called off.

In the aftermath of the Iranian mission, a special operations advisory panel was established to analyze and critique future plans. A joint anti-terrorist task force with integral SEAL, Delta, and air components (including Helicopter Task Force 160 and USAF Special Ops assets) has been established. The forming of JSOC (Joint Special Operations Command) has also aided the anti-terrorist effort as well.

Despite reorganization, Delta still had helicopter problems on Grenada when delays in arriving choppers caused Delta's mission of assaulting Richmond Hill Prison to fail since the choppers were driven off by alerted gunners. In addition to seeing action on Grenada, members of Delta have carried out some missions at U.S. embassies where they have provided special security and offered advice, not to mention gaining inside information about the layout and operations should a rescue ever have to be launched. Delta operatives have been widely used in such protective duties in Central America. It was reported that members of Delta or other U.S. anti-terrorist specialists took part in the Venezuelan assault on a hijacked DC-9 in July 1984, but this report is probably false. In December 1984, Delta returned to the Middle East when it was ready to assault a Kuwaiti airliner which had been hijacked; the hijacking resulted in the deaths of two Americans. Had the airliner left Iran, Delta was poised to strike. Then, in June 1985, the hijacking of a TWA flight saw Delta sent to Cyprus for a possible assault.

A key part of Delta's capability lately has rested with the men of SEAL Team 6, which specializes in anti-terrorism and which works as part of Delta. SEAL 6, which was established in November 1980, is highly classified but appears to have about 100 SEALs assigned, all top-notch volunteers from other SEAL Teams. SEAL Team 6's specialties reportedly include thwarting terrorist attacks on oil rigs in the Gulf of Mexico and on U.S. ships.

Members of SEAL Team 6 receive intensive firearms training as do other members of Delta. Among the SEALs' special armament are the S&W Mark 22, Model O suppressed 9mm auto, the H&K M54A1 SMG, and the MAC-10 SMG. Reportedly, SEAL Team 6 also has some pretty exotic weaponry as well. SEAL 6 has worked especially closely with the SAS and SBS. Normally, SEAL 6 assaults in four-man teams. Members of the unit were employed on Grenada, where they infiltrated in and protected General Sir Paul Scoon until they were relieved.

Another element of JSOC (Joint Special Operations Command) which has at least some anti-terrorist commitment are the 1st, 2nd, and 3rd Ranger Battalions. In certain situations where a larger raid is deemed necessary, the Rangers might be sent in to support a rescue. On Grenada, for example, the 1st and 2nd Ranger Battalions carried out a combat jump and rescued American medical students.

Finally, it should be noted that a SOT (Special Operations Training) Course is run at Ft. Bragg. This course runs three weeks and introduces members of Special Forces to hostage rescue techniques. Normally, each Special Forces battalion will have one company which has received such training and which has a limited HRU responsibility. Within such a company, one or two teams will specialize so that they can train foreign HRUs or, in certain situations, carry out rescues.

FBI HRT

Although in certain extreme situations, Delta or even the Rangers might be employed on an anti-terrorist operation in the United States (Delta, for example, was on alert during the 1984 Olympics), their responsibility normally is only to deal with acts of terrorism outside of the United States. Primary HRU responsibility within the States rests with the FBI's national "Super-SWAT" or "Hurt" (Hostage Response Team). This 50-man unit received intensive training and was in place for the 1984 summer Olympics and the 1984 presidential conventions. Members of the unit receive training in close-quarters battle, rappelling, assault tactics, entry techniques, hand-to-hand combat, negotiations and terrorist psychology, communications, the use of high-tech surveillance equipment, sniping/counter-sniping, and other standard anti-terrorist skills. At least some members of the unit are skilled pilots or scuba divers or possess other specialized skills.

The FBI uses assault tactics very similar to the SAS, even to the extent of wearing balaclavas and black utilities. In the FBI "Killing House," live "hostages" drawn from FBI instructors are used in live-fire scenarios à la SAS.

Like the SAS, the FBI "HRT" assaults with the H&K MP5 or MP5SD as its primary weapon. Sophisticated low-light optics are available should they be needed. Also in SAS-style, a Browning Hi-Power in a drop holster is worn as the secondary arm (or primary arm in certain types of assault). FBI snipers (who are very good and score right up with Delta's and the Secret Service's snipers in special matches held between the units) are equipped with the USMC M-40A1 system.

The "HRT" ranked among the best HRUs in the world as of 1984, but, unfortunately, the unit is no longer a full-time HRU and only comes together for periodic training. Admittedly, FBI resources are somewhat strained with the increased emphasis on spy catching, but constant training and constant readiness is much harder to maintain when a unit is broken up and given other assignments. Since major terrorist incidents, fortunately, are not common occurrences, keeping a highly skilled HRU together for extended periods is often a problem, especially in Third World countries. A nation with the resources of the United States, however, should be able to maintain a 50-man unit in a constant state of readiness. Admittedly, Delta is available as a backup, but due to legalities, the FBI should really handle terrorism within the United States. In addition to the national FBI "HRT," regional FBI offices normally have their own HRUs as well, though these units are not full-time and draw from agents with other duties and are assembled only for training or for a callout.

OTHER U.S. HRUs

Within the United States federal law-enforcement community, there are various other HRUs. The Secret Service, for example, maintains an HRU, as does the U.S. Marshal's Service. Even the National Park Police have one. The latter unit actually has a pretty good reputation and might see action should a national monument be occupied by terrorists. Because of the threat of nuclear terrorism, the Dept. of Energy maintains its own SWAT teams, as well as a specialized unit known as NEST (Nuclear Emergency Search Team).

NEST has various tasks, but one of them would include locating hijacked nuclear devices using sophisticated technology. The author has heard some rumors of a well-trained national Department of Energy (DOE) SWAT team to work with NEST to recover nuclear materials, but there has been no confirmation. The FBI "HRT" and Delta are both trained for such a scenario, though, and could provide an assault unit. NEST is skilled even at detecting a nuclear device hidden in a large urban area should terrorists manage to steal one or smuggle one into the country.

NEST is headquartered in Germantown, Maryland, and keeps nuclear-materials detection equipment pre-positioned at the following sites: Nevada Operations Office, Department of Energy, Las Vegas, NV; Aerial Measurements Operations, EG&G, Inc., Las Vegas, NV; Washington Aerial Measurements Dept., EG&G, Inc., Andrews AFB; Los Alamos National Scientific Laboratory, Los Alamos, NM; Lawrence Livermore National Laboratory, Livermore, CA; and Sandia National Laboratory, Kirtland Air Force Base, Albuquerque, NM. This detection gear is palletized for instant deployment aboard U.S. Air Force aircraft.

NEST has actually been deployed to counter threatened terrorist use of nuclear devices, though reportedly these callouts proved to be false alarms.

Local hostage situations in large metropolitan areas will be dealt with by local SWAT or hostage response teams. The Los Angeles team is probably the best known, though many other municipalities have very good units.

The problem the United States may have in dealing with terrorism may not be the lack of effective anti-terrorist units; Delta, the FBI "HRT," and NEST—not to mention the others—are quite well trained. The problem, instead, may be political. Prior to the Los Angeles Olympics, for example, there was a great deal of squabbling over whether the FBI or the Los Angeles SWAT team would handle a terrorist incident. Some of

Delta's problems in the past have stemmed from inter-service rivalry and a cumbersome chain of command.

The best anti-terrorist forces in the world are only effective if they can be brought into action quickly and with a clear directive. Fortunately, the administration of Ronald Reagan has shown a willingness to take decisive action (as in Grenada, the forcing down of the hijackers of the *Achille Lauro,* the air strike on Libya) and has been willing to structure the joint anti-terrorist forces at Fort Bragg so that intelligence, assault capability, and transport are much more integrated. All of these are positive steps, as was the forming of the FBI "HRT." If the U.S. is serious about combating terrorism, especially within its own borders, however, the FBI "HRT" should remain as a full-time national HRU, not a part-time one.

CHAPTER 6

The Rest of the World

In the preceding chapters, I have discussed the anti-terrorist capabilities of the United States and the European nations. This chapter will discuss world HRUs by evaluating those about which I have some knowledge. Strictly speaking, this section could not be labeled "Third World HRUs" because nations such as Israel, Australia, Canada, and Japan are more closely tied to the nations of the West. As far as anti-terrorist capability goes, Israel and Australia have the premier HRUs outside North America and Western Europe.

Most of the units discussed in this chapter, however, are those of Third World nations. The competency level of such units varies greatly, and even some units which were at a reasonably high level of readiness when created and trained will have declined through lack of use, misuse, or being split up and assigned to other units. One of the greatest difficulties in countries with such limited budgets and limited pools of manpower is keeping a purpose-trained HRU from being shifted to other duties or diluted. "Internal security" and VIP protection are the tasks most frequently assigned to such units; though both of these missions can validly fall under an HRU's venue, concentration on these duties can adversely affect training for the rescue mission. A note on weapons and equipment is important, too. Many Third World HRUs, even if they could afford sophisticated weapons and equipment, would have problems maintaining it.

Most HRUs covered in this chapter received training from one or more of the HRU superstars, with Israel, GSG-9, SAS, and GIGN being the largest exporters of HRU training. As a result, training, tactics, and weaponry will often be very similar to those of the unit's mentors. A few of these units have carried out operations; where possible, such ops will be discussed under the individual units.

AUSTRALIAN SAS

The Australian SAS was given the responsibility for providing Australia's national HRU in 1979. The original anti-terrorist unit was then doubled in size in 1980, when responsibility for protecting offshore oil and gas platforms in the Bass Strait was added to other HRU/ anti-terrorist duties. The unit is based at the headquarters for the 1st Australian SAS Squadron at Swanbourne near Perth.

The selection process is quite similar to that of the British SAS, as is CQB training. The Australians, for example, have their own "Killing House" with 360-degree shooting capability. One difference between it and the 22nd SAS is that the Australians tend to leave a man on anti-terrorist/HRU duties longer—a year rather than six months—before rotating him to other assignments within the Regiment. Like the British SAS, the Australians carry out very rigorous training in CQB, using live "hostages" in some Killing House scenarios, reportedly including some political notables. Upon joining the anti-terrorist troop of 1st SAS squadron, the new man is put through an intensive three-month course in CQB and sniping to hone his already good shooting skills. Training is also carried out in abandoned buildings in Perth and on Quantas and other aircraft. Parachuting and rappelling are standard skills for all members of the unit, while many members are also scuba, small boat, mountain, HALO or other specialty trained.

The Australian SAS HRU has done exchange training with the British SAS, GSG-9, the New Zealand SAS, and the Americans (among others).

Weapons for the Australian SAS include the Browning Hi-Power, the L1A1 and M-16 rifles, and MP5 SMGs. Parker-Hale Model 82 sniper's rifles are believed used. Since the Australian SAS has such wide anti-terrorist responsibilities, a large array of high-tech surveillance equipment, special scaling ladders, and other hardware is available as well.

NEW ZEALAND

The New Zealand SAS Squadron handles HRU duties for that country. As with Australia and Great Britain, the selection process for the NZSAS is such that very highly skilled candidates are thus available. Exchange with the other SAS units has aided training and tactics. Armament is also similar to the other SAS HRUs.

CANADA

Canada's national HRU is the Emergency Response Teams of the Royal Canadian Mounted Police. This unit was formed in 1977 and is organized and trained along GSG-9 lines. There are about 300 men assigned throughout the country. In addition to GSG-9, which helped form the unit, the RCMP ER Teams have trained with the FBI HRT and the Finns. Armament includes S&W Model 10 .38 Special revolvers and reportedly SIG-Sauer 9mm autos, M-16 assault rifles, Winchester Model 70 sniper's rifles, and fighting shotguns. Individual provinces have their own units which fulfill the SWAT mission, while the RCMP would handle "political" situations involving terrorists and certain criminal cases.

SOUTH AFRICA

Two police units act as HRUs for South Africa. The South African Police Special Task Force under the Security Branch is the primary national HRU. This unit was organized in 1977 and is parachute qualified and trained in CQB, assault tactics, and other HRU skills. After the disasters at the Israeli embassy and the Sandton Bank Siege, this unit was reportedly revamped and upgraded. Their "Killing House" is now reportedly quite sophisticated with intensive critiquing of videos after individuals go through a scenario. Since recruits for this unit have all seen some service in "operational" areas, all are fit and somewhat experienced. Reportedly, some of the expertise from the old Rhodesian "Urban Emergency Units" has carried over to the Special Task Force as well. The second unit is the Special Task Force of the South African Rail and Harbor Police. This 75-man unit is primarily an anti-hijacking unit trained to retake hijacked trains, ships, etc. Reportedly, this unit, and probably the other one, has received training from Israel. Training is very similar to the other police HRU, but there is a special emphasis on assaults against trains or other modes of transport. Weapons include 9mm auto pistols, Uzis, Stens, and R-1 rifles.

JAPAN

Although the author has heard rumors of a super secret Japanese national HRU trained almost as "modern ninja," the only HRUs known to exist for certain are the Police Special Action Units. These units are basically SWAT units assigned around the country in various police districts. At least one unit is reportedly trained for operations at Haneda and Narita Airports in Tokyo. It is likely that these units are selected from the

Riot Police, which in Japan are an especially fit elite. These units are actually rather well trained in close combat and entry tactics and have had training with the Germans, French, British, and Israelis, among others. Weapons include Smith & Wesson .38 Special revolvers and Beretta rifles.

KOREA

South Korea's principal HRU is the 707th Special Mission Battalion of the Army Special Warfare Command. Although this unit is composed of six teams, only two of them are really trained for the HRU mission. These HRU teams were created in 1982 and reportedly total about 120 men, though this number is probably being increased as preparations progress for the 1988 Summer Olympics.

The unit is located at Songnam City outside Seoul and is known to have received training from GSG-9 and the United States, among others. Members of the unit are already special forces qualified and thus have received training in parachute, rappelling, hand-to-hand (all are probably black belts or above in taekwon do), weapons usage, and demolitions. Additional training in combat shooting, breaching, assault tactics, and other HRU skills is received after being selected for one of the two teams. Korean special forces troops are known for their toughness, and the members of the 707th Special Mission Bn are even tougher than the norm. Their training facility is one of the most sophisticated in the world and reportedly includes a comprehensive shooting area to develop CQB skills. There are also indications that members of the 707th Special Mission Battalion have seen quite a lot of operational deployment against North Korean infiltrators. Armament for this unit includes the Colt Government Model .45 auto and the CAR-15.

Counterterrorist Special Attack Unit

The Counterterrorist Special Attack Unit (Tae-t'ero-Tukkong-Tae) of the National Police (probably drawn from the Combat Police, a heavily armed border patrol unit) consists of about 80 men and has received training from GSG-9. This unit is reportedly used extensively for VIP protection assignments as well as HRU tasks. The unit is headquartered at Yongin in Kyonggi Province and has a well-equipped training facility where members of the unit receive extensive close-combat training with and without weapons. Members of this unit are equipped with H&K MP5 SMGs, .38 Special revolvers, and the M-21 sniper system. Like the Army unit, this one is reportedly being expanded in preparation for the 1988 Olympics.

SINGAPORE

Singapore's HRU is the Police Tactical Team, which is a well-trained SWAT team of about 100 men. This unit is organized and trained along GSG-9 lines and has received training from GSG-9, the SAS, and the Israelis. Training includes normal HRU skills, including CQB, assault tactics, breaching, and rappelling. This unit is considered to be quite competent and is usually rated among the best in the Far East. In certain situations, members of the unit may also be used for VIP protection. Hijackings at either Changi or Seletar Airport would also be handled by this unit. The pistol used by the unit is the H&K P7, and the principal assault weapon is the H&K MP5. The sniper's rifle is reportedly also German.

For larger-scale operations, the 1st Commando Battalion of the armed forces has received some HRU training from GSG-9, Australian SAS, Israel, the Nationalist Chinese, and India.

HONG KONG

The Police Special Duties Unit (SDU) of the Hong Kong Police Tactical Unit provides HRU capability for the Crown Colony. This unit dates from the mid-1970s and has a strength of about 100 men. The unit is organized and trained along SAS lines; it has received substantial training assistance from the SAS and also the SBS since combat swimmer and small-boat skills are so important to an HRU operating in Hong Kong. Zodiacs and other craft for the SDU are provided by the SBU (Small Boat Unit) of the Police Marine Division. All members of the Special Duties Unit are among the most extensively trained police anti-terrorist "commandos" in the world; like the GIGN, they have received training in both scuba and parachuting. GIGN, in fact, as well as GSG-9 and the Royal Dutch Marines, has assisted in training the unit. Normal HRU skills are taught with emphasis on dealing with hijackings at Kai Tak Airport or in the harbor. As might be expected, members of the unit are well trained in the martial arts. Weapons include the Browning Hi-Power and the H&K MP5. This is a very professional and capable unit which grants Hong Kong a real deterrent to terrorists.

INDONESIA

Indonesia has a very diverse group of units assigned the HRU mission to a greater or lesser extent. The unit which has been in existence the longest is the SATGAS GEGANA (counterterrorist task force) of the Indonesian National Police. There are approximately 100 men, plus a 60-man support company assigned to the unit, with at least some of the personnel being military rather than police. The unit is stationed at Kelapa Dua, about 20 kilometers from Jakarta. All members are airborne qualified and have received training in combat shooting, hand-to-hand combat, rappelling, entry techniques, and other HRU skills. Among the unit's armament are M-16 rifles, M-1 sniper's rifles, and AK-47 assault rifles.

Detachment 81

Detachment 81 (also known as the Special Commando Team) of the KOPASSANDHA–Komando Pasukan Sandhi Yudhi (the Indonesian Army Special Forces) is another unit with an HRU mission. This unit, with a strength of about 100 men, is organized along GSG-9 lines and has received training from that unit and from the SAS. Members of this unit have already received special forces, airborne, scuba, and other special training during their qualification for the Special Forces but, upon selection for Detachment 81, receive additional CQB and other HRU training. Among their weapons are H&K automatic pistols, H&K carbines or SMGs, and FN FALs with folding stocks. Detachment 81 reportedly carried out the assault on the hijacked Indonesian airliner in Bangkok.

Other Units

Other units include SATGAS ATBARA, which is the Antiskyjacking Task Force of the Indonesian Air Force. This unit was formed in 1976 and is drawn from KOPASGAT, the Air Force Rapid Reaction Force, which is a special ops unit trained in counterinsurgency as well as air-base defense. There is a combat swimmer unit in the Indonesian Navy, the KESATUAN GURITA, which may have had some HRU training, but normally anti-terrorist tasks involving naval facilities and, especially, oil rigs would fall to the JALA MENGKARA of the Indonesian Marine Corps.

PHILIPPINES

There are various units in the Philippines which are

charged with the hostage rescue mission. Perhaps the best is the Air Force's AVESCOM (Aviations Security Commando), which is charged with the anti-hijacking mission. This unit was formed in 1972 and has small teams drawn from the following squadrons: 801st in Manila, 802nd in Luzon, 803rd in the Visayan Islands, 804th in Mindanao, and the 805th at the Manila Airport. The first four units are about equivalent to U.S. police SWAT teams in training, while the unit at the airport is the primary HRU. The SAS has given some training to the airport unit and probably to some of the other units. Recently, this unit has performed special close protection duties for President Aquino. Primary armament for the AVESCOM is .45 auto pistols and M-16 rifles.

Other Units

The Philippine Constabulary maintains another reasonably well-trained unit in the LRF (Light Reaction Force) based at Camp Crane in Manila. This unit has four 30-man teams in a company and has received training from the British and Australian SAS and from some U.S. anti-terrorist experts. Training is in the usual HRU skills, especially close combat and entry techniques. Armament includes the Colt Government Model .45 auto, M-16 rifle, and sniper's rifle.

Two other units also exist. The Army Special Warfare Brigade has a SOG (Special Operations Group) which was formed in 1978 and which has received training from the Israelis. The INPFF (Integrated National Police Field Force) also maintains 16 companies trained to carry out low-level hostage rescue operations in criminal or other cases. These companies are trained in a manner similar to U.S. SWAT teams.

THAILAND

There are various HRUs in Thailand, and it is difficult to decide which one is the premier unit. The last aircraft hijacking was reportedly handled by a special HRU of the Royal Thai Air Force. It can probably be assumed that this unit is especially trained to handle aircraft hijackings and receives training in CQB, breaching, and other skills specifically geared to retaking an airliner. Their weapons include Browning Hi-Powers, Uzi SMGs, and Mauser Model 66 sniper's rifles.

Among the other assorted units trained for anti-terrorist/HRU duties are a small unit of the Royal Thai Navy's SEALs, a unit of the 1st Army's 1st Division (which has trained with GSG-9), a unit of the Army's Special Forces, and Special Operations and SWAT units of the Royal Thai Police.

PAKISTAN

Pakistan has a very well-trained HRU consisting of about 175 men within the SSG (Special Services Group) of the army. This unit, being a military special forces unit, has already received airborne, special forces, and other specialized training before joining the HRU company. Upon selection for the anti-terrorist mission, however, members receive additional training in combat shooting, demolitions, hand-to-hand combat, rescue tactics, breaching and other entry methods. Training has been provided by the SAS and, reportedly, this unit assaults in SAS style. This would seem to indicate the use of the Browning Hi-Power and the H&K MP5, but the author has been unable to confirm this and, in fact, has information that the unit has, in the past at least, been armed with the P-38 pistol. This unit carried out a rescue operation in September 1981, during an airplane hijacking at Lahore and performed quite professionally.

INDIA

India has one of the best HRUs in Asia in the SCTU (Special Counterterrorist Unit). This 100-man unit was formed in 1979 and is drawn from India's highly trained para-commandos. This unit is part of the Special Frontier Force based at Sarsawa Airfield in Uttar Pradesh. All members of the unit are already airborne and commando qualified and thus have received a lot of training before joining the unit. After being selected for the SCTU, they undergo additional training in CQB, breaching, rappelling as it applies to HRU, use of special-purpose pyrotechnics, terrorist methods, and other HRU skills.

During the last couple of years, the unit has been deployed at various times to deal with Sikh hijackings or other Sikh incidents.

The primary assault arms for the unit are the Browning Hi-Power and the Sterling SMG. AR-18 and AK-47 assault rifles are also available.

SRI LANKA

The Sri Lankan anti-terrorist unit is the Army Commando Squadron, which is based at Ganemulla near Colombo. Since the Sri Lankan international airport is at Colombo, this is a logical place to base this unit. Candidates must have first attended the 34-day basic commando course, which is primarily designed to test the student's physical ability, initiative, and resourcefulness. Top graduates of this course who volunteer for the Commando Squadron receive an additional three months of advanced training, which includes Close Quarters Battle (CQB) with weapons and without, land navigation, rappelling, demolitions, first aid, jungle tactics and survival, rock climbing, and physical conditioning along with assault tactics and other HRU skills. The final exercise in the advanced training course is a 150-mile march through the jungle in five days or less. This unit received anti-terrorist/HRU training from an eight-man SAS team in July 1981. Israel has also given training assistance. Weapons include the Browning Hi-Power, H&K MP5, and AK-47.

MALAYSIA

The primary HRU is drawn from the Unit Timpaan Khas (Special Strike Unit) and/or Unit Tindak Khas (Special Action Unit) of the Royal Malaysian Police. The unit was originally formed in 1969 as an EOD (Explosive Ordnance Disposal) unit, but its duties were expanded to include hostage rescue missions. The SAS has given assistance in training for this mission. Members of the unit are drawn from the Police Field Force and Federal Reserve Force. Strength is about 50 men who have received training in the normal HRU skills. Armament includes .38 Special revolvers, M-16 rifles, and shotguns. Browning Hi-Powers, H&K MP5SD SMGs, and Beretta Model 70 5.56mm rifles have also been reportedly used with Malaysian anti-terrorist forces, though it is possible that this is the armament of the small (reportedly only ten men) army unit trained in anti-terrorist tactics. This army unit is probably drawn from the Special Services Regiment.

COLOMBIA

The primary HRU for Colombia is the GOES (Special Operations Group) of the Policia Nacional. This unit was originally formed to deal with kidnappings, which have been an endemic problem in Colombia. Negotiating and investigation were actually stressed in training, more so than HRU tactics and skills. The course for the GOES lasts three months at the National Police training facility. Spanish experts, presumably from GEO, have also worked with the unit. Assault tactics, breaching, and CQB skills are rudimentary at best, though. The unit is organized into ten-man teams deployed at various points around the country. Weapons include .38 Special revolvers and 9mm Browning Hi-Powers, various types of SMGs, and FN FAL rifles. For explosive entry, dynamite or other improvised demolitions are used!

The army also has ten-man teams known as GAES (Anti Extortion and Kidnapping Groups) which are assigned to each brigade. As their name implies, they are also concerned primarily with preventing or dealing with kidnapping; however, they have had some minimal HRU training.

The Colombian Air Force has two GAJDA teams, also of ten men each. These units work at airports and are presumably trained in the anti-hijacking role.

In evaluating Colombian HRU capability, the siege at the Justice Palace should be borne in mind. Colombian "anti-terrorist" forces assaulted, killing all the terrorists as well as more than 80 hostages. It must be understood, though, that since no terrorists survived the assault, the Colombian government considered the assault to be a success.

HONDURAS

The national HRU for Honduras is the COE (Comando de Operaciones Especiales) of the Honduran Army Special Forces Command. This unit was formed in 1983 and has a strength of about 60 men. The unit is trained by U.S. military advisors and draws upon airborne- and ranger-qualified volunteers who then receive additional training in hostage rescue, anti-terrorist, and counterinsurgency tactics. Among the weapons in use by the unit are the Browning Hi-Power 9mm auto pistol, Uzi SMG, CAR-15 and Galil 5.56mm assault rifles, Remington 700 and M-21 sniper's rifles, and Remington 1100 shotguns. Some of these shotguns have had the barrels cut back to 14 inches or less for taking out door hinges and for use in confined spaces.

Another HRU reportedly in existence is the "Cobras" Political Squadron of the FUSEP (Public Security Forces). This unit is also airborne qualified and has received SWAT-type training.

BRAZIL

Brazil has a relatively small HRU (about 25 to 30 men), which is part of the Army's Special Forces. This unit, known as Projecto Talon, was formed in the early 1980s and draws on recruits who are already trained in special forces skills. Additional hand-to-hand, combat shooting, rappelling, breaching, and assault skills are taught after a member is selected for the unit. Weapons include .357 Magnum revolvers (the author is not sure whether they are Smith & Wesson or Taurus), M-16 rifles, and sniper's rifles. It is also quite likely that the INA SMG has seen at least some usage.

ARGENTINA

The Argentinian Special Counterterrorism Team is known as "Halcon 8" (Falcon 8) and was formed in 1978 for the World Cup, which was held in Argentina. This unit, which has a strength of about 40 to 45 men, is part of the army and falls under the supervision of the Commando School. All members of the unit are airborne and commando qualified, with many HALO trained. HRU skills are added after the men are selected for the unit. Reportedly, assault weapons include the Argentine version of the Browning Hi-Power and the PA3-DM 9mm SMG. FN assault rifles are also used.

VENEZUELA

Venezuela's anti-terrorist unit is the Special Intervention Brigade, which was formerly a counterinsurgency unit that assumed HRU duties in 1978. Initial training was received from GSG-9 and later from the Israelis. The unit receives a combination of special operations/ HRU training but includes the usual—close combat, instinctive shooting, rappelling, explosive entry, and other skills. Because of Venezuela's oil revenues, this unit is equipped a bit more lavishly than many other

Latin American ones and is also trained to deal with oil-field incidents. Armament includes the Browning Hi-Power, H&K MP5, Ingrams, Uzis, FAL rifles, M-16 rifles, and, reportedly, a British sniping rifle.

The unit was deployed to El Salvador in May 1979, to rescue the ambassador at the Venezuelan embassy there, but the incident was resolved before an assault was necessary. Then, in July 1984, the unit carried out a successful assault in Aruba on a hijacked airliner and rescued 79 passengers. All of the hijackers were killed in the assault. There are indications, in fact, that the primary reason all hijackers were killed was so that none were around to talk to the press since it is possible that the hijackers had carried out the operation to try to force the Venezuelan government to pay them for covert operations carried out under government auspices. Obviously, this version would be officially denied.

ECUADOR

HRU duties in Ecuador are handled by the 200-strong Army Puma Unit. This unit was formed in 1980 and originally received training from the Israelis, later receiving additional training from the United States. The training is relatively extensive—six to eight months—and members of the unit tend to be of high caliber, being drawn from the Army's Special Forces and the Navy's SEALs. Twenty-five members of the unit have also trained with GEO. Among the weapons used are the Browning Hi-Power and the M-16.

CHILE

Chile has three HRUs in existence. The first is the *Grupo de Operaciones Especiales*—GOPE—of the Carabineros, a national police force. This unit, formed in 1979, is comprised of about 50 men and is one of the better trained units in Latin America. Airborne, scuba, assault tactics, CQB, breaching, rappelling, and other standard HRU skills are taught to the unit. Training assistance has come from GSG-9, Israel, and South Africa. The unit is reportedly using German weapons, probably the H&K MP5 and the P9S or P7.

Another anti-terrorist unit, which is also quite competent, is the *Unidad Anti-Terrorista*—UAT—which is drawn from the Carabineros and the army. Formed in 1980, this unit is comprised of about 100 men who are airborne and commando qualified before joining the unit. This unit also receives additional special training in hand-to-hand combat, quick reaction shooting, breaching, and other HRU skills. Israel and South Africa have both supplied training assistance. There is another unit, known as *Cobra,* which consists of about 50 men. Its special responsibility is toward the diplomatic missions in Santiago. It is not clear, however, if this is a separate unit or part of UAT. Weapons include the Uzi SMG, the CA-75 pistol, and the Galil 5.56mm rifle.

A third highly secret unit, known as *FACH,* is part of the Air Force. It may be surmised that this unit is trained in the anti-hijacking/sky marshal role, but this is not certain.

KENYA

Anti-terrorist capability within Kenya rests with the GSU (General Services Unit) Recce Company of the Kenya Police. This unit has received training from U.S. experts, among others, and is rated as quite competent. There has reportedly also been at least some contact with Israeli anti-terrorist experts and perhaps the SAS. Contact with the Israelis goes back at least a decade for the GSU since the unit provided security for the Israeli C-130s after the Entebbe operation and continues to provide special security for El Al flights landing at Nairobi. The Recce unit would, of course, respond to any hijackings or other hostage situations at the airport. Training includes a combination of HRU skills, such as breaching and assault tactics, rappelling, hand-to-hand combat, combat shooting, use of special-purpose explosives, ambush/anti-ambush, and helicopter insertions.

The unit's handgun is the Browning Hi-Power, while the principal assault weapon is the Uzi SMG. Sterlings and Stens are also in the inventory. The Remington 700 sniper's rifle is used, as is the Remington 870 fighting shotgun. Since the unit's mission also includes dealing with insurgents (such as the old Mau Mau threat), heavier armament is also included, such as the FN FAL and G-3 assault rifles, FN-MAG 58 LMG, the 66mm LAW, and the M79 40mm grenade launcher.

ISRAEL

Since Israel has traditionally termed any actions against the PLO and many actions against the confrontation states "anti-terrorist," it is difficult to limit Israeli anti-terrorist forces by calling them "hostage rescue units." The rescue of hostages is only one of their duties, which have frequently included retaliatory or preemptive strikes and assassinations.

Generally, Israeli anti-terrorist capability is traced to Unit 101, which was established in 1953 to carry out cross-border reprisal raids into Jordan or other neighboring states from which Palestinians were infiltrating Israel. Due to criticism of the draconian measures used by Unit 101, the unit was soon "disbanded," though in actuality it was merged with the Israeli Paratroop Battalion, which assumed the responsibility for raiding and reprisals during the 1950s and Sixties.

With the increase in terrorist acts after the stunning Israeli victory in the Six Day War of 1967, a more specialized unit—the Sayaret Matkal (also known as the General Staff Recon Unit or Unit 269)—was formed directly under the command of the Chief of Israeli Intelligence. This unit's strength during the later Sixties and early Seventies was approximately 200 men divided into units with a strength of roughly 20. Selection was normally from top army recruits with great competition to serve in the unit. Some members of the paratroops and naval commandos (combat swimmers) were also selected for the unit.

Training emphasized infiltration; desert operations; close combat with firearms, knives, and bare hands; languages (most spoke at least Hebrew, English, Arabic, and one other language); parachuting; communications; demolitions; rappelling; small boat usage; and often scuba. Many training exercises were in actuality carried out in enemy territory. In fact, much training was carried out on-the-job during raids across Israel's borders. Only about one-half of the recruits made it through training and selection satisfactorily.

Primary weapons for the Sayaret Matkal included the Uzi SMG, Galil assault rifle, and AK-47 assault rifle. The Beretta M51 9mm pistol was also used, though the primary handgun was the Beretta .22 auto. Special-purpose explosives or other equipment was available as needed.

To counter the attacks on El Al aircraft, members of Sayaret Matkal were trained as sky marshals and rode El Al airliners. In December 1968, members of the unit carried out a retaliatory raid for skyjackings when 40 of them hit Beirut Airport and blew up 13 Arab aircraft. During the War of Attrition, members of Sayaret Matkal were used to carry out raids into Egypt against military targets. In fact, as Sayaret Matkal evolved, it handled various types of special operations in addition to anti-terrorism. In this aspect, the unit was similar to the SAS.

In May 1972, however, the Sayaret Matkal carried out the first successful assault on a hijacked airliner. A Sabena 707 had been hijacked to Israel with ten crew members and 90 passengers aboard by four Black September terrorists. Disguised as mechanics, members of Sayaret Matkal assaulted the plane, killing two hijackers and wounding another and freeing all of the hostages except one who had been killed during the assault.

In September 1972, Israel wanted to send a Sayaret Matkal assault team to Munich to rescue the Israeli Olympic athletes taken hostage by Black September, but was denied permission. In retaliation for the murder of these athletes, Israeli hit teams were sent after high-ranking Palestinians. Members of Sayaret Matkal were reportedly on these teams. In April 1973, Sayaret Matkal also carried out raids in Beirut to assassinate key Palestinian leaders and destroy PLO headquarters there. In October 1973, however, Sayaret Matkal once again saw action as special ops troops during the Yom Kippur War.

Sayaret Matkal's reputation was somewhat tarnished in May 1974, when the PDFLP (Popular Democratic Front for the Liberation of Palestine) seized a school at Ma'alot in Israel. Sayaret Matkal was eventually sent in to assault, during which they killed all three terrorists, but 22 hostages were killed and 60 injured during the assault. Following the raid, an analysis showed many mistakes had been made. The attack had been delayed until the last minute and some of the value of surprise was therefore lost; the assault team hit the wrong floor of the building, thereby losing more time; and phosphorous grenades were thrown, causing the assault forces to hesitate while the smoke cleared so they could see.

In the aftermath of Ma'alot, there seems to have been some changes made in the Israeli anti-terrorist forces, though the General Staff Recon Unit seems to still be in existence and to have certain responsibilities. For internal hostage rescue operations, a special unit of the Israeli Border Police was established in 1975 with a strength of about 150. This unit is broken into 24-man platoons, which are broken into 12-man teams. Each team is broken once again into two six-man elements. This six-man element is the basic operational unit and includes a medic, a demolitions expert, and two snipers among its operatives. This unit receives an intensive four-month training course.

Weapons for the Border Police HRU include Beretta 92SB and Browning Hi-Power pistols, M-16 rifles, Steyr and Mauser 7.62mm sniper's rifles, and Uzis. A certain amount of surveillance gear and special-purpose pyrotechnics are available, though not as much as in some of the other HRUs such as GSG-9. There has been excellent cooperation, by the way, between GSG-9 and the Israeli anti-terrorist units; hence, it is likely that a lot of GSG-9 technology has been made available to the Israelis.

The Entebbe rescue in June 1976, of course, made the world aware of Israel's anti-terrorist capabilities. Though the General Staff Recon Unit was involved in the operation, however, the actual assault force was drawn from the 35th Para Brigade and the Golani Commandos. "Anti-terrorist" ops have continued through the 1980s in Southern Lebanon with the General Staff Recon Unit, the Paras, and the Naval Commandos all involved.

SAUDI ARABIA

The 3,500-man Special Security Force, which was established in 1971, has ostensibly had the HRU function since 1979. It has received training from GIGN and GSG-9, among others. Probably the best unit in the country, however, is the much smaller 40-man unit in the National Guard. Armed with the Browning Hi-Power, H&K MP5, M-16, and Remington M-700 sniper's rifle, this unit has received extensive training from U.S. experts.

After the hijacking of a Saudi L-1011 (in which the plane burned and the hijacking was covered up), reportedly, sky marshals have been trained and more emphasis has been put on training to retake a hijacked airliner. It should also be noted that Saudi policy is that no negotiations will take place to free any member of the Royal Family taken hostage by terrorists. Finally, it should be mentioned that GIGN gave special training to members of the Saudi National Guard in 1979 when they had to assault to retake the Great Mosque from radical Moslem terrorists.

BAHRAIN

The small oil-rich state of Bahrain has an HRU known as U-Group, which is part of the Public Security Force under the Minister of the Interior. This unit came into existence in the early 1980s and was trained by the British SAS. Its officers are, in fact, British, mostly "former" SAS, while the NCOs and troopers are Pakistanis "formerly" with that country's SSG (Special Service Group).

The unit is trained along SAS lines, and reportedly all members are airborne and scuba qualified. HRU training includes extensive CQB, breaching techniques, and insertion techniques. The unit has a strength of approximately 60 men, with two 25-man assault teams as the primary operational arms. These are probably broken into either four- or five-man elements. As part of the support staff, there is also a maritime section, an important element since Bahrain is surrounded by water.

Primary weapons for U-Group include the Browning Hi-Power, various versions of the H&K MP5 (which in SAS fashion is the primary assault weapon), H&K 91 assault rifles, and Remington Model 700 sniper's rifles. FN-MAG machine guns, 12-gauge fighting shotguns, and Carl Gustav 84mm rocket launchers are also in the armory, though the latter would not normally be used in hostage rescue situations!

This unit has carried out joint exercises with the SAS and with GSG-9, and it is rated as very competent by these units. The unit has integral Land Rovers, boats, and other equipment so that it does not have to rely on outside sources. The author is not aware of the status of U-Group's helicopter support, however, though the unit is trained in helicopter insertions, including rappelling from choppers.

There is another unit within the Bahraini Defense Force consisting of about 100 men which also has an anti-terrorist mission, but it is secondary to U-Group and would probably be used for containment in a major hostage situation.

JORDAN

The national anti-terrorist unit for Jordan is part of the 101st Special Forces Battalion. The HRU was initially trained by the SAS and still maintains strong ties with Hereford, but the unit now carries out its own training program. Although the entire 101st Battalion initially seems to have received HRU training, a 100-man unit, probably considered an S.F. company, now has the hostage rescue mission. This company is broken into three assault teams, with each team consisting of three assault elements and a sniper team. One team is always on alert. This unit was created in the mid-1970s and saw action in 1977 when the Intercontinental Hotel was occupied and had to be assaulted.

Armament consists of Browning Hi-Powers, H&K MP5s, Steyr SSG 7.62mm sniper's rifles, M-16 5.56mm assault rifles, and fighting shotguns.

There is also a special airport anti-hijacking unit highly trained as sky marshals and for aircraft assaults. This unit, which is based at Queen Alia International Airport, numbers about 500 and is considered quite competent. Reportedly, this unit has included female sky marshals in the past. Armament is very much the same as for the S.F. unit, but the anti-hijacking unit is also equipped with suppressed (silenced) .22 pistols for use aboard aircraft.

OMAN

Primary HRU duties rest with the Sultan's Special Force, which is officered by former British and Rhodesian special forces personnel, including a large number of SAS. NCOs are also reportedly contract personnel from British and Rhodesian special forces units. Enlisted personnel include Dhofaris. The unit was originally formed in 1977 as a counterinsurgency force but now also has the counterterrorist responsibility. The unit has approximately 500 members, with the HRU elements formed into 18-man teams stationed around the country at critical points and at the airport. This unit is reportedly armed with the Browning Hi-Power and the H&K MP5 for assaults, though the author has not confirmed this. The Sultan's Special Force is normally rated one of the best in the region.

The Royal Omani Police Special Task Force also has been trained for the HRU role. This unit has British contract officers and consists of approximately 300 men divided into five assault elements of about 60 men each. This unit reportedly assaults with Steyr AUGs as its primary arm. Overall, this unit is not rated too highly and would probably only carry out containment duties in a serious situation, while the Sultan's Special Force would actually assault.

One final unit which should be mentioned is the Omani combat swimmer unit, which has about 30 members commanded by a former British swimmer. The unit has trained with the SAS and Sultan's Special Force and might be called in for certain tasks should a tanker be hijacked or some other operation require their special skills. Armament includes S&W 9mm autos and the Steyr AUG.

TUNISIA

In 1982 a unit known as the Groupement de Commando of the Garde Nationale was formed as an antiterrorist unit. Like France's Gendarmerie, the Garde Nationale is a hybrid military/police unit with national responsibilities. The unit is reportedly about 100 strong and has been extensively trained in airborne, scuba, close combat (armed and unarmed), assault tactics, and other HRU/anti-terrorist skills. U.S. anti-terrorism experts have helped train this unit, and it is likely that there has been some contact with GIGN. This unit is now known as the GN Special Forces, though its mission remains the same. Weapons used by this unit include Browning Hi-Powers (two per man in assault teams), Beretta M12 SMGs, FN FAL 7.62mm rifles, Winchester M1200 fighting shotguns, and the M-21 sniper's rifle. Reportedly, S&W Model 19 .357 Magnum revolvers, FN-MAG LMGs, and Steyr AUGs are also available to the unit if needed.

MOROCCO

After the occupation of the Grand Mosque in Mecca, the Moroccans created an HRU in 1980. The unit is known as the GIGN, standing for the same as the French GIGN, which helped form and train the unit and still gives assistance. GSG-9 and the SAS have also helped with training. The Moroccan GIGN is comprised of 50 men, who are relatively well-trained in HRU skills. Their martial arts training is quite good, mostly due to a Korean martial arts instructor permanently assigned to the unit. Among GIGN arms are S&W .38 Special and .357 Mag. revolvers, Beretta 9mm autos, Star 9mm autos, Llama 9mm autos, and Browning 9mm autos; Uzi SMGs; and AK-47 assault rifles.

SUDAN

The principal HRU in the Sudan is the 144th CTU (Counter Terrorist Unit) which was established in 1980. The SAS, Egypt, the United States, and others have given assistance and training in basic hostage rescue techniques including CQB, assault tactics, explosive entry, sniping, rappelling, etc. Their armament consists of the H&K P9S and MP5 as principal assault arms.

Members of the Bern HRU are shown at right prior to the taking down of the Polish embassy in Bern, Switzerland, which had been occupied by terrorists.

Below: Ulrich Wegener, the Commander of GSG-9 at Mogadishu, is pictured at left with the crew of the hijacked Lufthansa flight and German officials. He is carrying a Smith & Wesson revolver.

Members of the "Pagoda Troop" of the 22nd SAS are shown going through the windows of the Iranian embassy. Note the anti-flash hoods, gas masks, and H&K MP5s, most notably the MP carried by the trooper at the rear which has a light affixed to it.

The "Pagoda Troop," above, enters the Iranian embassy through its windows during the Princes Gate Operation.

Left: "Pagoda Troop" members test various ladders for use during an aircraft assault.

22nd SAS members are shown above practicing train assault skills, wearing anti-flash hoods and carrying H&K MP5s with lights mounted and sighted to the bore. The trooper in the center is carrying an extension magazine.

At right, a "Pagoda Troop" member is shown in full CRW (Counter Revolutionary Warfare) kit. A spare magazine for the Browning is carried on his right wrist, while a low-slung Hi-Power holster and spare MP5 magazine pouch are worn on his left leg.

Britain's SBS (Special Boat Squadron) has anti-terrorist responsibility for the North Sea oil fields as well as other situations. Shown at left are two SBS members coming ashore during a recce mission. The point man is carrying a silenced Sterling SMG.

Among the best HRUs in the world is the Australian SAS, two members of which are shown below.

A crack Royal Marine Commando unit, including a heavy contingent of SBS, guards the North Sea oil rigs from terrorists. The unit known as Comacchion Company is trained for all sorts of assaults on a seized oil rig.

Wearing a balaclava, a member of the Spanish UEI HRU (left) is armed with an H&K MP5 with special night optics and a .357 Magnum revolver.

An H&K MP5 and H&K 9mm autos are carried by members of the Spanish GEO HRU (below). Their berets are dark brown, and the men are shown wearing a rappelling harness.

Armed with the Steyr-AUG assault rifle, members of Austria's Cobra Unit are shown doi
security duties.

Members of the FBI's HRT administer to a freed "hostage" during an exercise (left). Note the H&K MP5 and Browning Hi-Power carried by the HRT member.

HRT members are shown below during their approach prior to a practice assault. Tires are used as a backstop for shooting in certain training scenarios. Note the gas masks, black utilities, MP5s, and SAS-style leg holsters.

GIGN members are all extremely fit and are shown above wearing para brevets on their right breasts.

At right, GIGN men are pictured free-climbing a building during a training exercise.

A member of the 75th Infantry (Ranger) is pictured following a parachute insertion, a method which might be used to send in Rangers for a large-scale rescue (such as that conducted on Grenada).

This member of the U.S. Army Special Forces undergoing sniper training at the Marine Sniper School would be a likely candidate for Delta because of his special skills. Note the heavy-barrelled sniper's rifle and the "Ghillie" suit he wears for camouflage.

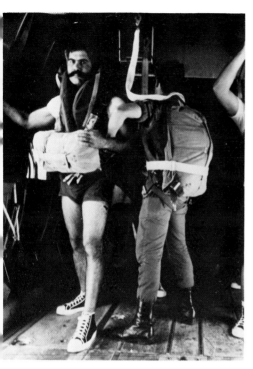

The Israeli Naval Commandos are shown at left prior to a "wet jump." The Naval Commandos have carried out many anti-terrorist ops and have contributed members to the 269 and other Israeli anti-terrorist units.

Israeli paras, such as the one shown below, made up the assault force at Entebbe.

Members of the SAS assault team prepare to rappel down the rear face of the Iranian embassy during the assault at Princes Gate. Note the sledge-hammers which proved necessary when the frame charges could not be used on the windows.

In certain hostage situations, Soviet "Spetsnaz" might be employed to carry out a rescue.

Members of the Royal Dutch Marine Close Combat Unit (right) arrive by chopper prior to the assault on Train 747, armed with Uzis and wearing ballistic vests.

Two members of the Tunisian GCGN prepare to assault (below). Members of GCGN's assault teams carry two Browning Hi-Powers.

The G-3 and AK-47 assault rifles are also available. It is not clear if the G3A3ZF functions as the unit's sniper's rifle or not. The Special Forces Company of the Sudanese Airborne Brigade also seems to have at least some anti-terrorist capability, and it was this unit which carried out the rescue of four Western missionaries on 8 July 1983 from the South Sudanese Liberation Front. This operation was carried off quite professionally as the Special Forces assault unit was landed by chopper to carry out its assault on the plateau where the missionaries were held. The combination of hitting quickly, using jet aircraft for a diversion, and surprise allowed for a successful rescue.

LEBANON

Because of the unstable situation in Lebanon, it is very difficult to say what the current state of the anti-terrorist capability is, especially since in Lebanon it may be very difficult to come up with a definition of "terrorist" which is acceptable to all members of a unit. As of 1983 there was a unit in the Lebanese Army known as "Moukafaha" which was charged with the counterterrorist/special operations mission. This unit was trained much along Ranger lines, with a limited amount of HRU skills included. The later Tactical Strike Force received more traditional HRU training, including operations in urban areas, assault tactics, breaching methods, close combat, and rappelling. This unit reportedly received training from the U.S. Special Forces.

Weapons for the Tactical Strike Force included Star 9mm and Kassnar 9mm pistols, the SIG M-540 5.56mm assault rifle, the Remington Model 700 sniper's rifle, and Remington 870 fighting shotguns. Due to the situation in Lebanon, it is unclear what the status of this unit is when this book went to press, though the unit is reportedly still in existence.

EGYPT

Due to two disastrous assaults, the reputation of Egypt's HRUs does not stand very high. The original unit was Saiqa ("lightning"). In March 1978, two PLO assassins gunned down a close friend of Egyptian President Anwar Sadat in Nicosia, Cyprus. After the killing, the two terrorists initially barricaded themselves, along with 30 hostages, in a hotel but later were bused, along with 15 hostages, to Larnaca Airport to board a Cypriot airliner for transport to another Arab state. After flying around the Middle East and being refused permission to land in numerous countries, the DC-8 returned to Cyprus. In the meanwhile, Egypt had dispatched 54 members of Saiqa to Cyprus, though the Cypriot authorities had been informed a group of negotiators—not an assault force—was on its way. Despite the fact that it appeared negotiations had been successful to free the hostages, the Saiqa commander, Gen. Shukry, ordered the Egyptians to assault, resulting in a firefight with Cypriot National Guardsmen that left 15 Egyptians dead and could have resulted in the deaths of all of the hostages.

The second abortive operation was even more of a disaster. In September 1985, EgyptAir Flight 648 was hijacked to Malta. This time, Force 777, Egypt's current anti-terrorist unit, was sent to Malta to carry out a rescue if needed. In this case, the Maltese agreed to the assault, though reluctantly. The Egyptian assault force was on the ground for 11 hours waiting for orders to go in, but did not seem to have used the time gathering intelligence about the whereabouts of the hijackers or their armament despite the availability of released hostages and the possibility of using surveillance devices. Five passengers had been shot prior to the Egyptian assault, which would certainly justify going in. However, the Egyptians appear to have made other mistakes. In addition to not gathering proper intelligence, they also probably assaulted too early since they went in around 2015, a time the terrorists were likely to be alert. Dawn is usually a much better time for an assault, and since no passengers had been shot for some time, it is possible that a dawn assault would have been more successful. The Egyptian covert entry was proper as they went in through the cargo doors initially. Other 777 members were on the wings ready to blow the emergency hatches. Unfortunately, the Egyptian choice of a diversion was poor since they had decided to detonate a charge in the cargo hold beneath the cabin as a distraction prior to the assault teams going in through the escape hatches. The terrorists, however, heard the cargo bay door being opened and were alerted. When the assault began, no stun grenades were used either. The 777 teams just went in. Between bullets, explossions, and smoke inhalation (the most predominant cause of death), 57 hostages were killed during the assault. The slowness of the assault—90 seconds, at least, which is three to four times the length a successful assault should last—combined with the fact Egyptian sharpshooters stationed outside the plane seemed to have fired on escaping passengers in the mistaken notion that they were terrorists, added to the death toll.

Force 777 was created in 1978 and is subordinate to the Army Commando Command with which it shares a headquarters in Cairo. Current strength for Force 777 is about 250 men. All members of the unit are volunteers who have already received airborne commando training.

Physical conditioning for the unit is excellent, though their training in marksmanship and assault tactics needs to be improved, as the raid on Malta unfortunately illustrated. There seem to be some command and control problems with the unit, too, which inhibit its effectiveness. Since training assistance has been given by GSG-9, GIGN, and U.S. experts, tactics should have been taught and no doubt were, but the day-to-day exercises may leave something to be desired.

In the Egyptians' favor, it should be pointed out that

they have carried out successful assaults, as at Luxor in 1975, for example, when ironically the same airliner involved in the Malta hijacking was successfully assaulted. All passengers were rescued.

Weapons used by 777 include the 9mm Helwan pistol (the Egyptian version of the Beretta 951) as the primary handgun, though some S&W Model 19 .357 Magnums have been used, as have some Makarovs. The Egyptian version of the AKM is the primary assault weapon, though Ingram SMGs are also in the inventory. Various sniper systems have been used.

CHAPTER 7

How the Units Stack Up

I am reluctant in many ways to rate the various HRUs, but I do feel it would be beneficial to have some idea which units are the best in the world. As a result, I have set up six criteria for evaluating national HRUs and assigned values from 5 (the highest) to 1 (the lowest) for each criteria. Obviously, there is considerable subjectivity in my evaluation, and the scores assigned are not only relative but somewhat arbitrary.

The perfect score on the six criteria would be 30, and one unit—the British SAS—achieves this mark. GSG-9 comes close with 29. Any unit making it into my ratings of the Top Ten, however, should be considered extremely competent and extremely capable. I doubt there will be much disagreement with my evaluation of the SAS and GSG-9 as being the creme de la creme of the world's HRUs. These two units are generally accepted as the ultimate pros in the field, and they've earned that place in the minds of most of their contemporaries around the globe.

There may well be some disagreement about my next four—Australian SAS, GIGN, Israel, and Delta.

They're all very, very good, but in my opinion, I'd put them just a shade below the SAS and GSG-9. In actuality, however, these units are roughly equivalent. Then, there is the final four of my top ten, which includes the Spanish UEI & GEO, FBI, Italian GIS, and Royal Dutch Marines. I emphasize again that all ten units are very, very good. Nevertheless, I have a feeling that photos of yours truly will soon turn up on the faces of terrorist targets in a few "killing houses" when my ratings get around!

The following are the six categories I have rated each unit on:

COMMAND AND CONTROL

A good HRU needs a streamlined command structure which will keep it from being mired in so much bureaucracy that it takes forever to send the unit into action. The decision makers must also have the will to use the unit if necessary. The New Zealand SAS, for example, though a very competent unit, gets very low marks on this criteria due to the current government in Aukland, which hasn't shown much backbone. To get high marks on command and control, an HRU needs to have an effective command and control structure, backed up by a government with the will to use the unit when necessary. The only point GSG-9 lost in my markings was based on my perception that the German government does not match the British government of Margaret Thatcher in its willingness to combat terrorism. This criteria is an extremely important one since no unit, no matter how good, can do well if it's hamstrung politically.

TRAINING

To keep the myriad skills needed by a top HRU sharp, intensive and constant training is absolutely necessary. As a result, it was difficult to score well in this category unless a unit has a full-time and varied training program. Units with too many other tasks to train for may also have been marked down on this criteria.

PERSONNEL/SELECTION

An HRU is only as good as its personnel; therefore, this criteria rates the selection process used by the units and the quality of the personnel thus selected. To achieve a perfect score, a unit should have a selection procedure which results in personnel who are intelligent, dedicated, outstanding physically, have initiative, and are capable of operating individually or as part of a team. The higher the quality of the manpower pool the unit has to draw from, the higher, generally, the caliber of the HRU.

WEAPONS AND EQUIPMENT

In simple terms, this criteria evaluates the unit on its choice of weapons and equipment and on its overall technological backup. If weapons are dictated by national pride, for example, as opposed to efficiency, the unit is likely to get marked down. The lack of specialist equipment, such as assault ladders, pyrotechnics, or commo equipment, might also rate a unit down.

INTELLIGENCE AND RESEARCH

In planning an operation, an HRU must have access to sound intelligence and should have its own integral intelligence staff to convert raw intelligence into a form usable by the HRU. A good unit should also have its own research capability to improve equipment, discover available equipment which can be applied to its mission, evaluate lessons learned from previous hostage rescue/anti-terrorist operations, and formulate contingency plans for possible rescue scenarios. Optimumly, all members of the unit will have some expertise in these skills in addition to having specialist personnel.

VERSATILITY/RESOURCEFULNESS

Because of the need for instantaneous decisions and because few hostage rescue missions are carried out exactly as planned, the members of such a unit must immediately be able to adjust to unforeseen circumstances and find solutions to unforeseen problems. Ruses and deceptions are often useful in distracting terrorists during an assault, and the good hostage rescue unit must possess personnel who can think on their feet to come up with such ruses.

Below, then, are the ratings with an explanation of why I rated each unit as I did:

1. BRITISH SPECIAL AIR SERVICE

Command & Control	5
Training	5
Personnel/Selection	5
Weapons/Equipment	5
Intelligence/Research	5
Versatility/Resourcefulness	5
	30

The SAS's well-known selection system ensures top-quality recruits who then receive intensive training in anti-terrorist skills, especially combat shooting and other close quarters battle skills. Because of the system of rotating squadrons into the HRU slot, the SAS keeps such skills sharp but does not allow them to go stale. As with anything it undertakes, the SAS shows great professionalism in the way it handles the hostage rescue mission. Backing up the excellent selection and training procedures is the SAS Ops Research Unit, which ensures that proper, though often simple, equipment is available to perform the task. If possible, the SAS prefers that an item perform multiple tasks. One of the keys to SAS success is simplicity. At Princes Gate, for example, members of the assault team carried a high-tech entry device known as a sledgehammer! When the frame charges could not be used, the sledges proved invaluable. The SAS applies "Ockham's Razor" to complex problems and uses the simplest workable solution. If necessary, they can be tricky, but normally they rely on a sound plan, well-executed with minimum razzle-dazzle. The fact that the British frequently run full-scale anti-terrorist exercises involving the prime minister, all the way down to the assault teams, greatly enhances this command and control rating.

2. GSG-9

Command and Control	4
Training	5
Personnel/Selection	5
Weapons/Equipment	5
Intelligence/Research	5
Versatility/Resourcefulness	5
	29

The only point GSG-9 was marked down on was command and control since the German government has seemed a bit softer on terrorism lately. Even in the past, there was reluctance to use GSG-9, and currently it appears that such reluctance could keep GSG-9 from being committed immediately if needed. If possible, GSG-9 would get even higher marks on weapons and equipment since the unit has often been the forerunner in developing new hardware or developing tactics for employing existing hardware. GSG-9's experience with the H&K MP5, for example, helped establish this weapon as the premier anti-terrorist arm in the world.

The West German Border Guard (the *Bundesgrenz-schutz*) has tough selection standards itself, and GSG-9 then runs its own selection course to select the best of this already elite group. Add the outstanding GSG-9 training which trains unit members to think as well as act, and one can understand the unit's high marks on selection, personnel, and training. Through the excellent computer system in Wiesbaden, which keeps track of terrorists and other data, GSG-9's intelligence sources are excellent and the unit's technical and intelligence staff is trained to maximize any information supplied to the unit.

3. GIGN

Command and Control	4
Training	5
Personnel/Selection	5
Weapons/Equipment	4
Intelligence/Research	4
Versatility/Resourcefulness	5
	27

GIGN gets top marks on training because it is so intense and well-rounded. Each man in the unit, for example, is trained as a sniper, parachutist, and combat swimmer. Selection is also rigorous and assures the unit of intelligent, physically outstanding, well-motivated recruits. Like GSG-9 and SAS, GIGN has an already well-trained manpower pool to choose from in the Gendarmerie Nationale. GIGN is marked down a little on command and control because of some scandals involving the unit and because of a slight softening on France's part against terrorism. The unit is also downrated slightly on weapons and equipment due to the choice of the Manurhin revolver which, though an excellent weapon (and a French one), is not as practical as a large-capacity autoloader. The relative neglect of the SMG on GIGN's part also affected this rating. Though still ranked third on my list, there are many experts who would rank this unit substantially lower, feeling the unit has declined greatly since the departure of Capt. Prouteau.

4. AUSTRALIAN SAS

Command and Control	4
Training	5
Personnel/Selection	5
Weapons/Equipment	4
Intelligence/Research	4
Versatility/Resourcefulness	5
	27

For many readers, my ranking of the Australian SAS so highly may be a surprise, though for anyone who knows this unit the surprise may be that they're ranked as low as third/fourth. I have rated the SAS only a 4 on command and control because it is not certain how willing the Australian government would be to use the unit on external ops. Likewise, I have rated the unit down slightly on equipment and intelligence. Anyone who has served with the Australians knows they are a resourceful people and, hence, the unit's high rating on this characteristic, especially when considered along with the excellent SAS selection and training process which inculcates resourcefulness. The cooperation between the British SAS and Australian SAS is a real advantage for both, though it may occasionally mean that the Australians rely a lot on the British for intelligence, research, and equipment. Still, with the slight decline in GIGN's prestige lately, the Australian SAS is probably, in actuality, the number three unit, with GIGN dropping to fourth.

5. ISRAEL

Command and Control	5
Training	3
Personnel/Selection	4
Weapons/Equipment	4
Intelligence/Research	5
Versatility/Resourcefulness	5
	26

Israel has, of course, shown excellent will in the fight against terrorism. The Israeli counterterrorist force—the Sayaret Matkal—also has a clear and direct command structure which is very responsive and lets the unit be brought into action quickly if needed. As a result, I would probably rate this unit tops in command and control. I have rated the Israelis down on training for two reasons. First, as at Entebbe, certain hostage rescue missions have been organized on a rather ad-hoc basis. Second, members of the "anti-terrorist" units are often assigned other missions so that their HRU skills may suffer as a result. Though the personnel of this unit is of very high caliber, politics have occasionally entered into the selection process to assure the inclusion of members of important families. As a result, I've downgraded the selection process slightly. Intelligence and versatility are other real assets of Israeli anti-terrorist forces, the former because of the capabilities of the Mossad and the latter through the necessity of substituting resourcefulness for manpower or hardware in many instances.

6. DELTA

Command and Control	3
Training	5
Personnel/Selection	5
Weapons/Equipment	4
Intelligence/Research	4
Versatility/Resourcefulness	4
	25

No doubt some friends of mine in Fayetteville will be disappointed at ranking only sixth in my ratings, but much of this low rating can be blamed on past bureaucratic infighting and ass-covering. That I even rated Delta a "3" on command and control is attributable to the reorganization of the command structure after the failed Iranian mission and the will of Ronald Reagan to fight terrorism. Delta's record of employment so far has shown a lot of muddled thinking on the part of higher level commanders and poor support for the unit. Training, personnel, and selection for Delta are all excellent. Even the British SAS, which has had a lot to do with Delta organization, selection, and training, has learned from Delta's training techniques. Intelligence, research, and versatility have all been marked down slightly due, once again, to bureaucratic impediments. Although Delta has access to much high-tech hardware, I have marked the unit down slightly because of the over-complicated accurized .45 autos used by the unit and its use of the M-3 "Grease Gun" (rather than a more effective anti-terrorist SMG such as the MP5). The members of Delta are very good, but bureaucratic considerations may inhibit the unit's effectiveness.

7. UEI/GEO

Command and Control	3
Training	4
Personnel/Selection	4
Weapons/Equipment	4
Intelligence/Research	4
Versatility/Resourcefulness	4
	23

I have combined both of Spain's HRUs for purposes of evaluation. In actuality, most experts rate UEI as superior to GEO, though both are quite good. UEI is especially strong on technical backup and realistic shooting training, which helps the ratings on training and equipment. Both units have relied heavily on other European units for assistance in training, especially GSG-9, the SAS, and GIGN. As a result, I have not rated either unit at the maximum on research and intelligence. Training is quite thorough, and the selection process is good for both units; therefore the marks are relatively high in those categories. UEI especially has shown resourcefulness in operations against the ETA, though details cannot be discussed. Like many other European governments, the Spanish one has not taken the toughest possible stance on terrorism which, combined with the split chain of command due to the existence of both units, lowers the rating for command and control.

8. FBI HRT

Command and Control	3
Training	3
Personnel/Selection	4
Weapons/Equipment	5
Intelligence/Research	4
Versatility/Resourcefulness	3
	22

The FBI rating is down a few notches from what it would have been a couple of years ago due to the fact that the unit is no longer a full-time HRU; this change in status has in turn adversely affected its training rating. I have also downrated the unit on command and control because of the various jurisdictional disputes which have arisen and which could delay deployment in an emergency. Personnel are quite good due to the FBI's high standards, and weapons and equipment are excellent. Intelligence and research capability are also quite good since the FBI is in charge of domestic intelligence and thus can supply information to its own unit. Although the individual FBI agents may be versatile and resourceful, the unit—as its name implies—is part of the federal bureaucracy, and that does not encourage individual or group resourcefulness. The FBI HRT is still very good, but not quite as good as it was circa 1984.

9. GIS

Command and Control	3
Training	4
Personnel/Selection	4
Weapons/Equipment	4
Intelligence/Research	3
Versatility/Resourcefulness	3
	21

GIS is a very competent HRU, even though I have not given it the highest rating in any category. Italian anti-terrorist capability seems to have peaked with the freeing of General Dozier and the subsequent decimation of the Red Brigades. Italy's will to fight terrorism seems to have eroded somewhat since that point, however, as illustrated by the hesitancy in dealing with the *Achille Lauro* hijacking and the unwillingness to take a stand against Libyan terrorism. Add to those factors the diversity of anti-terrorist units in Italy, and one can see the reasons for only average marks on command and control. The personnel of GIS, selected from the Carabinieri, are quite competent, though, due to good selection and training procedures. Italian anti-terrorist intelligence gathering has left something to be desired in the past, and this failing carries over to GIS, which doesn't have a strong research capability, either. GIS is a very good HRU, but its intelligence backup and the questionable will of those in the chain of command who will have to make the decision to commit the unit if necessary might be improved.

10. ROYAL DUTCH MARINES

Command and Control	3
Training	4
Personnel/Selection	3
Weapons/Equipment	4
Intelligence/Research	3
Versatility/Resourcefulness	4
	21

When sent in on operations, the Royal Dutch Marines have gotten the job done, and that's the bottom line. Still, the Dutch Marines Close Combat Unit has labored under some disadvantages which account for my rating it tenth. The Dutch authorities, for example, have proven overly hesitant to commit the unit and overly worried about the lives of terrorists, thus hindering the unit's effectiveness and possibly endangering the Marine assault teams. The unit's training is good, but the selection procedure isn't as rigorous as that of some other units. The Dutch Marines, admittedly, have a good pool of manpower to select from, but the caliber is not as high as that of the SAS. Initial selection, as a result, needs to be a bit more rigorous. I have given the Dutch Marine Close Combat Unit good marks on weapons and equipment due to its arsenal of high-tech devices and experience with using them. Their resourcefulness has also been proven in such instances as the use of the jets during the assault on Train 747 to keep the hostages' and terrorists' heads down during the assault.

In considering my rankings of the top ten HRUs in the world, a couple of points should be borne in mind. First, these are my subjective rankings and should be considered as such. Secondly, all ten of these units are very professional, very competent, and very highly trained. The countries they protect can be justifiably proud of the men who give so much of themselves to serve in these crack HRUs, and the citizens of these countries can feel a little more confident in the wake of the terrorist threat knowing they are protected by the pros of any of these ten units, regardless of whether I rated them number 1 or number 10.

I hope in writing this book I've managed to give the reader some insight into the skills and capabilities of the HRU and some understanding of what an incredibly difficult job the HRU faces when it has to "go in." Not only do the lives of hostages rest on the shoulders of the anti-terrorist "commando," but national prestige does as well since the whole world is watching when an HRU swings into action. If they're successful, they're heroes and their country goes into a state of instant euphoria. A clear warning has been sent to terrorists ("don't screw around with our citizens unless you want to face the SAS, or GSG-9, or GIGN"). But, if the HRU fails, hostages die, national prestige suffers, and perhaps a few terrorists consider that country to be a slightly softer target.

This book, therefore, is dedicated to those guys who right now are on alert in Hereford, at Fort Bragg, at St. Augustin, at Maisons-Alfort, and dozens of other places around the globe making it a little safer place for me to be writing this book and you to be reading it.

APPENDIX I

Weapons and Equipment

To fully appreciate how an HRU operates, one must have at least a rudimentary understanding of the weapons and equipment with which it carries out a mission. This chapter contains a discussion of the principal weapons and equipment used by the HRU operator to gain intelligence about his objective, to gain access to the objective, to carry out his assault, to attack the terrorists, and to protect himself during the assault. I have tried to keep the discussion of weapons and equipment relatively basic while still including enough discussion of the subject to offer what I hope will be useful information for those working in the anti-terrorist field. Such a compromise will obviously prevent my discussions from becoming overly technical, though technical details are explained where such explanations may help enhance the appreciation of the functioning of certain pieces of hardware. In some cases, I have provided a minimal amount of information regarding certain equipment or excluded certain information due to security considerations.

HANDGUNS

For the member of an HRU, the handgun serves a dual purpose. It is a backup arm which is available should the SMG malfunction or be lost during an assault. It can also be used as a primary assault arm in certain confined situations or when an SMG is not considered selective enough. Frequently, the pointman during an assault will also be armed with a handgun to allow him more freedom of movement and one hand free for other tasks. The pointman, for example, may need one hand free to handle an inspection mirror, carry a stun grenade ready for action, or to open doors. There are certain scenarios where the assault troop may have to engage a target one-handed. In this case, the handgun is particularly useful. GIGN, especially, trains in the use of the Manurhin .357 with one hand while rappelling. During approaches in cramped quarters, such as crawl spaces and aircraft baggage compartments, the handgun may prove especially valuable. Sometimes an HRU member will be infiltrated into a site as a waiter, aircrewman, driver, et al., and a concealable handgun may be the only applicable weapon. A good example of this occurred in one European country when a single individual was holding two hostages in a hotel room. Posing as a waiter bringing food, an HRU member gained admittance and killed the hostage-taker with two shots from his Hi-Power.

With all but the most highly-trained HRU, the handgun may actually be the best assault weapon because the operative must consciously pull the trigger each time he fires, thereby countering any tendency to fire wildly and forcing target selection. Units such as the SAS, GSG-9, Delta, UEI, and FBI HRT are very well-trained with their SMGs and can use them surgically, but my experience with many Third World HRUs is that they do not train consistently at quick reaction, precise shooting with their SMGs, and thus the handgun is a better assault weapon for them. Unfortunately, due to machismo, many units which should be using the pistol as their primary assault weapon choose the SMG instead.

When the handgun is chosen for HRU employment, however, especially in the assault, the correct weapon must be chosen. GSG-9's use of the S&W Model 36 .38 Special at Mogadishu, for example, proved to be a real mistake.

In many countries, the anti-terrorist commando may be in danger of assassination if his identity becomes known; therefore, the handgun and skill with that weapon may be important to self-preservation. I know of at least two cases, in fact, where Third World HRU members were attacked by terrorists and managed to save their lives through quick action with their pistols. In one case, the man and his family were returning home when two assassins opened up with SMGs. He managed to kill one of the terrorists with his Hi-Power and force the other to break off his attack. One of his children was slightly wounded, but due to his quick reaction everyone else was unharmed.

A very large percentage of HRU members around the world, whether police or military, are armed 24 hours a day, and more than one has used his handgun when theoretically off-duty. One example which comes to mind concerns a member of Delta who shot and killed an intruder in his home just before being deployed for the Iranian hostage rescue mission.

The handgun is important, too, when the HRU is assigned peripheral duties such as VIP protection or sky-marshaling. The handgun is also used undercover, as on ops in Ulster by the SAS.

The diversity of handguns in use is relatively wide, but a few stand out as superior for HRU usage. The handgun to be used by an HRU must be accurate and reliable. Normally, the semiauto 9x19mm with a large magazine capacity is the best choice, though the superior stopping power of the .357 Magnum or .44 Magnum may be called for in certain situations. Some

HRUs have accurizing/customizing performed on their pistols but normally such gunsmithing consists only of improved sights, trigger smoothing, and reliability enhancement.

Based on my own experience the best handguns for HRU usage are the following:

Browning Hi-Power

This 9mm autoloader is overwhelmingly the most popular pistol with HRUs. The Hi-Power's popularity stems from its excellent accuracy and reliability. It is also in the inventories of many military and police organizations around the world. In simple terms, its popularity stems from a combination of propinquity and excellent design.

The Hi-Power is a single-action, locked-breech auto of Colt/Browning type. Its 13-round magazine gives it good sustained fire capability. Overall length is 7.75 inches; weight is 35 ounces; and barrel length is 4.65 inches.

Beretta 92SBF

This double-action, locked-breech 9mm auto will gain even more acceptance with HRUs now that it is the USA's new service pistol. The 92SBF is highly reliable and accurate. The double-action, first-round capability not only aids in bringing the Beretta into action quickly, but it also enhances safety. Its magazine capacity of 15 rounds definitely gives the 92SBF enough firepower for HRU usage. Overall length for the gun is 8 1/2 inches; weight is 33 1/2 ounces; and barrel length is 5 inches.

SIG-Sauer P-226

This 9mm double-action, locked breech auto is my personal favorite for HRU purposes. Combining the best of Swiss and German technology, the P-226 is superbly accurate and reliable right out of the box. The fact that the P-226 uses so many stampings should not be taken as an indication of a lack of quality either. Overall length for the P-226 is 7.7 inches, weight is only 29 ounces (due to its alloy frame), and barrel length is 4 3/8 inches. As with the other top autos for HRU usage, the P-226 has a large magazine capacity—15.

CZ75

This Czechoslovakian double-action, locked-breech 9mm auto is an excellent one and can be used either as double action or single action. The CZ75 combines some of the best features of the Browning Hi-Power and the SIG P-210, which makes for an excellent pistol, both accurate and reliable. Overall length is 8 inches; weight is 35 ounces; and barrel length is 4 3/4 inches. The magazine capacity is 15. Probably more HRUs would use the CZ75 if it were not manufactured in a Communist country.

H&K P7M8

The P7 has two real points in its favor: It is very compact, and its unique squeeze cocker safety makes it very safe (with well-trained users) and very accurate. The squeeze cocker enhances accuracy since it allows each shot to be fired with a light, consistent trigger pull because the striker is cocked by the squeeze cocker rather than a pull on the trigger. The P7 is a 9x19mm. Overall length is only 6 1/2 inches despite a barrel which is just over 4 inches in length. Weight is 25 ounces. The standard P7M8 has an 8-round magazine capacity; for those wanting a larger magazine capacity, there's the P7M13 which holds 13 rounds. My recommendation would be for the P7M8 since the squeeze cocker alone adds bulk to the grip. With the larger magazine capacity, the grip may be uncomfortable for many.

H&K P9S

H&K's other widely used 9mm auto (also available in .45 ACP) is the P9S. The P9S is a double-action, delayed blowback auto with a magazine capacity of 9 rounds in 9mm chambering. Overall length is 7.6 inches; weight is 32 ounces; and barrel length is 4 inches. Although the P9S is an excellent auto, I would normally recommend one of the larger-capacity 9mm autos for HRUs.

Colt Government Model

Despite the fact that it has been in service for three-quarters of a century, the big Colt auto still has its advocates, some of them in HRUs. The greatest advantages of the .45 auto for HRUs are the .45 ACP round's knockdown power and its lack of penetration due to its lower velocity. Such a combination is highly desirable for a weapon likely to be used in an urban environment or aboard an airliner, a ship, or train. The Colt is a single-action, locked-breech auto with a magazine capacity of 7 rounds in .45 ACP chambering. (It's also available in 9x19mm and .38 Super chamberings as well.) With an overall length of 8 1/2 inches, the Colt weighs in at 39 ounces and has a barrel length of 5 inches.

Smith & Wesson 459

At the risk of sounding unpatriotic, I don't rate the 459 quite as highly for HRU usage as the other 9mm autos already discussed. Still, it is widely distributed, and it is a Smith & Wesson. The 459 is a double-action, locked-breech 9mm auto with a magazine capacity of 14 rounds. Its weight is only 27 ounces thanks to its alloy frame. Overall length is 7.5 inches, and barrel length is 4 inches. One of the 459's strong points is that it is extremely durable. Since it is also a Smith & Wesson, the 459 is sometimes easier to get law-enforcement HRUs to adopt rather than something considered more "esoteric" in bureaucratic minds.

Revolvers

A minority of HRUs employ some type of revolver, most often a .357 Magnum Smith & Wesson or Manurhin. In a few cases, the Smith & Wesson Model 29 .44 Magnum revolver is available for situations in which maximum stopping power is needed. The primary limiting function of revolvers for HRU usage is that they only carry 6 rounds and are slower to reload than an automatic pistol. They also tend to be far bulkier and heavier for an equivalent barrel length than an auto pistol.

SUBMACHINE GUNS

The SMG is normally the primary assault weapon for an HRU since it gives a lot of close-range firepower yet uses a pistol bullet—normally the 9x19mm or .45 ACP—which will not overpenetrate. In almost every major hostage rescue operation carried out within the last 15 years, the SMG has been the key assault weapon. At Entebbe, Train 747, Mogadishu, Princes Gate, and in many other assaults the SMG has been the instrument that effectively has helped terrorists die for their beliefs.

For HRU usage, the SMG must be capable of a high degree of accuracy in the hands of a skilled user since shooting will often be in a hostage situation where exact shot placement is critical. This accuracy is a combined function of the weapon itself and the user who must receive intensive training. So important is intensive training with the SMG (or any weapon for that matter) that there aren't really more than 15 to 20 HRUs in the world properly trained to use the SMG in the assault, yet many others employ the SMG as their assault weapon with somewhat questionable skill. Because the assault team may have to work quickly in confined quarters, the SMG must be as compact as possible, though normally the mini-SMGs are not acceptable. To enhance their effectiveness in low-light conditions, the SMG should have the capability for installing special low-light optics.

Although there are quite a few SMGs which are used by at least one HRU, there are really only three which are highly suited: the Heckler & Koch MP5, Uzi, and Beretta M12.

Though there are other SMGs which have achieved a limited acceptance with HRUs (such as the U.S. M3 and Ingram MAC 10, the Swedish K, the Walther MP-L, and the Czech Skorpion), the three SMGs discussed below dominate the field, with more than half of the major HRUs in the world using some version of the MP5.

H&K MP5

Overwhelmingly, the MP5 in its various configurations is the choice of HRUs. The 9x19mm MP5's roller delay blowback system allows excellent accuracy since the gun fires from a closed bolt, especially when used in three-shot bursts. The four aperture rotating barrel rear sight helps accuracy, too. Both 15- and 30-round magazines are available. The MP5 is available in three basic forms, two with telescoping or fixed stocks.

The basic MP5 is the MP5A2, which has an 8.85 inch barrel, a high-impact plastic stock, and a 750 RPM cyclic rate. The overall length on the MP5A2 is 26 3/4 inches, and it weighs 5.69 pounds. The MP5A3 is basically the same weapon but has a telescoping skeleton stock which brings its overall length down to 19.29 inches. There are three suppressed ("silenced") versions of the MP5—the MP5SD1, with no stock; the MP5SD2, with a high-impact plastic stock; and the MP5SD3, with a telescoping stock. The barrel on these three versions is 6 inches in length, and cyclic rate is lower at 650 RPM. Weight ranges from 6.17 pounds to 7.5 pounds. Many HRUs prefer one of these suppressed MP5s due to their lower cyclic rate and desirability of the lower sound level on certain operations (i.e., eliminating one terrorist without alerting his cohorts). The third version is the compact MP5K, which is normally used primarily on VIP protective assignments or covert entry situations. The MP5K has no stock, a 4.5 inch barrel, and a cyclic rate of 840 RPM. The overall length is only 12.8 inches, and the weight is only 4.4 pounds. Various special light mounts and night-vision optics are available for the MP5.

Uzi

The 9x19mm Uzi has been around since 1949. After the MP5, it is the most widely used SMG among HRUs. Due to the location of the magazine housing in the pistol grip and the bolt that extends forward over the barrel, the Uzi is surprisingly compact considering its 10.25-inch barrel. Overall length is, in fact, only 17 inches, but it is a relatively heavy weapon at 7 pounds 10 ounces. The combination of this weight and the relatively low cyclic rate of 550 to 600 RPM make the Uzi a relatively controllable weapon, for which 25-, 32-, and 40-round magazines are available. Both a wooden stock and a telescoping metal stock can be used, but most HRUs tend to choose the latter. Special light mounts are also available. Equivalent to the MP5K is the Mini-Uzi, which may be in HRU arsenals for VIP protection and certain other special scenarios.

Beretta M12

The third SMG which has received relatively wide acceptance with HRUs is the 9mm Beretta M12. Like the Uzi, the M12 saves overall length by having the bolt head recessed to go over the barrel. This system also helps to reduce muzzle climb. The M12 uses either a folding metal stock or a fixed wooden one, though the latter is rarely seen. The front hand grip and the pistol grip allow good control of the weapon in full-auto fire. The M12 is selective fire and can be fired quite quickly and accurately on single-shot mode if one so chooses. Overall length for the M12 with stock folded is only 16.4 inches, and weight is only 6 pounds, 8 ounces. The barrel length is 8 inches. Cyclic rate is a very controllable 550 RPM; 20-, 30-, and 40-round magazines are available for the M12.

SNIPER'S RIFLES

The sniper's rifle gives the HRU the ability to resolve certain hostage situations at long range, often with one shot. Tactically, the sniper is an invaluable element in the HRU since, unlike the assault team which must "go in," the sniper can wait for the hostage-taker to present himself as a target. HRUs normally have clearly defined procedures and guidelines worked out for the employment of snipers. Target identification and tracking, the "kill" order, and automatic kills (i.e., most snipers are authorized in certain situations to immediately kill a hostage-taker in their sights if the hostage is in imminent danger), communications, and other such details are clearly defined. Although there have probably been more hostage situations resolved by snipers (especially in criminal cases by police SWAT personnel) than by assault, the only one which stands out among national HRU operations is the simultaneous killing of the Djibouti bus hijackers by GIGN.

Snipers are normally selected for such characteristics as calmness, stability, judgment, patience, vision, and, of course, marksmanship. Many units try to pick nonsmokers, too, since smoking often has an adverse effect on marksmanship. The ability to observe and gather intelligence is another critical skill for the sniper since his vantage point and sophisticated optics will often enable him to relay critical information to the assault teams. Normally, snipers are trained in pairs in which one member is to operate as the observer and the other as the "shooter," though each man will be fully trained in both skills. By having the members of the team rotate on a long vigil, the fatigue factor is counteracted to some extent.

When snipers are being trained, they should always have the same rifle so that they can learn its idiosyncrasies and know exactly where the bullet will go. Likewise, the sniper should normally train with one specific load so that he will know its characteristics at various ranges and under various conditions. Training should be under different light and weather conditions, at different ranges, and using scenarios with the most lifelike targets possible and which duplicate different environments (i.e., buildings, airliners, vehicles, ships, etc.). Training should include exercises in observation, especially of detail. Maintenance of the rifle and its optics must also be stressed in training. Snipers should be trained in methods of covert infiltration as well as rappelling, scaling, and other skills which will enable them to reach their firing points undetected. Since the sniper's forte is delivering an unexpected deadly stroke upon command, it is very important that he remain covert until called upon. It should be pointed out, too, that the command given to the sniper should be short and clear. "Kill Target #2," for example, makes sure everyone understands what is required.

There are certain characteristics shared by most good sniper's rifles in use by HRUs: free-floating barrel, adjustable trigger pull, availability of a bipod, ability to shoot under 1.00 minute of angle (in simple terms, to put five shots center-to-center in less than one inch at 100 yards), a cartridge (usually 7.62mm NATO, though some HRUs are going for more powerful .300 Magnum rounds) able to reach out to 500 yards or more, and optics (preferably with integral range-finding capability) usable in varying light conditions and at varying ranges. A good sniper's rifle should be durable since it may take punishment during the approach to the shooting position. Traditionally, the sniper's rifle has been a bolt action, but many HRUs are switching over to highly accurate self-loading rifles which allow more rapid target acquisition should the sniper have to deal with multiple targets.

Among the various sniper/countersniper rifles and optics systems in use around the world, a few stand out as clearly superior. A short discussion of these follows.

Steyr SSG and SSG-PII

The SSG is a bolt action that comes equipped with adjustable butt pads and double set triggers. It is chambered for the 7.62mm NATO round. Unlike some sniper's rifles, the SSG does not have a truly heavy barrel but more of a medium heavy one. The stock is of Cycolac, and the gun is fitted with a detachable 5-round magazine. The standard scope for the SSG, which comes with quick detachable mounts that allow it to return very closely to zero when taken off and replaced, is the Kahles ZF69 six-power, which has a trajectory compensator designed specifically for the SSG. Also available for the SSG is the Kahles Hella, an eight-power low-light scope. This may be the most effective non-electrically assisted low-light scope in the world.

Steyr updated the SSG with the SSG-PII, which has an improved bolt, a single adjustable trigger, and a heavy barrel.

H&K PSG1

The PSG1 is a semi-automatic 7.62mm NATO rifle with a free-floating bull barrel and single adjustable trigger. Five- and 20-round magazines are available for the rifle. At almost 18 pounds unloaded, the PSG1 is no lightweight, but it is meant for precision shooting from a fixed position. The weight helps reduce recoil substantially as well. The stock itself has an adjustable cheek piece, pistol grip, and butt plate to facilitate exact fitting to the shooter. A bipod attaches directly to the fore-end, thereby eliminating the problems caused by pressure on the barrel by a bipod clamp. The standard scope is the 6x42 Hensoldt Wetzler, adjustable from 100 to 600 meters, which has a built-in battery-powered illumination unit for the crosshairs in low-light shooting.

This rifle/scope combo is not only accurate, but also very fast in engaging multiple targets.

Accuracy International PM

The PM is a bolt-action 7.62mm NATO rifle with a free-floating stainless steel barrel. It has an interchangeable, sealed, adjustable trigger, which can be switched between rifles. The bolt is designed so that the head does not have to be moved at all during its operation, thus allowing continuous observation of the target. The rifle is designed, in fact, so observation is constant through the recoil cycle as well. The rifle is equipped with a bipod and a retractable spike on the rear of the butt so that the rifle can, in effect, rest comfortably on a tripod during long periods of observation. This is a real plus for a rifle designed for HRU usage since the shot might not be offered or ordered for hours. It has a box magazine which will hold up to 12 rounds. Accuracy is excellent out to 600 meters or even further. Reportedly, at least a few examples of this rifle have been supplied in .300 Winchester Magnum to the SAS SP Team for longer range striking power.

The standard scope sight is the Schmidt and Bender 6x42.

SSG 2000

Produced by SIG Sauer, the SSG 2000 is a bolt action available in 5.56mm, 7.5mm Swiss, 7.62mm NATO, and .300 Weatherby Magnum chamberings. The stock is of straight-line type with a thumb hole and adjustable cheek rest and butt plate. A metal rail under the fore-end takes a tripod. The trigger can function as a set trigger or as a standard trigger. The bull barrel is equipped with a very effective muzzle brake which reduces muzzle flash and lowers and redirects muzzle jump. A detachable magazine holds four rounds. Like the H&K PSG1, the SSG is a heavy rifle at 14 pounds.

The standard telescopic sight is the Zeiss Diatal ZA8x56 or a Schmidt and Bender 1.5-6.0x42 Vario. The Sauer swing-in mount is standard and keeps a constant zero even if the scope is taken off and then put back on.

Mauser SP66

This 7.62mm NATO rifle uses the Mauser short-bolt action. The massive stock has an adjustable cheek piece and butt plate, a thumb hole, and a pistol grip. A flash hider/muzzle brake is fitted on the barrel. The magazine is integral with a 3-round capacity.

The standard telescopic sight is the Zeiss Diavari ZA 1.5-6x variable. A mount for night-vision optics is also included with the rifle.

H&K G3SG/1

This self-loading 7.62mm NATO weapon is that oddity, a fully automatic sniper's rifle. It is basically the G3 rifle with a select barrel, a variable set trigger, and an adjustable cheek piece on the stock. The standard telescopic sight is the Zeiss Diavari 1.5x-6.0x variable.

M40-A1

This 7.62mm NATO bolt-action rifle, based on the Remington 700, is the USMC sniper's rifle. It is also used by the FBI HRT. The fiberglass stock is fitted with a Pachmayr recoil pad. Its Remington trigger has a 4 1/2 pound pull. The telescopic sight used with the M40-A1 was originally a Redfield 3x-9x variable, but it has been replaced by the Unertl 10x. This rifle/scope combo is extremely accurate and durable.

WA 2000

This semi-automatic sniper's rifle from Walther is chambered for the .300 Winchester Magnum, 7.62mm NATO, or 7.5mm Swiss cartridge. The WA2000 looks very high-tech, and it lives up to its appearance. For one thing, the action is in the butt in "bullpup" fashion. The barrel is also unique, having a bulky, barrel extender which aids in cooling and a profiled barrel which is completely free-floating inside of a frame with rails above and below it. The upper rail takes the bipod and scope mount, and the lower rail takes the handguard, trigger group, and magazine housing. The magazine, by the way, holds 6 rounds. The location of the bipod on the upper rail allows the rifle to swing well from side-to-side since it is suspended between the legs. Like many of the better anti-terrorist sniper's rifles, the WA2000 is quite heavy—16 pounds to be exact. The stock which is attached to the frame has a rubber butt plate that is fully adjustable.

The standard sight for the WA2000 is the Schmidt & Bender 2.5x-10x56 variable, though the weapon is also intended for use with various low-light optics.

Parker Hale Models 82 and 85

Both of these are bolt-action 7.62mm NATO weapons. The Model 82 is highly accurate—0.5 minute of angle—and features a fully free-floating barrel. The walnut stock is adjustable with extension spacers. The Model 82 uses a single stage trigger adjustable for backlash, creep, and pull. The Model 85 is also highly accurate and very sturdy. It has an ambidextrous stock which is adjustable for length with butt spacers. It is also fitted with a fully adjustable bipod. The Model 82 has a 4-round capacity, while the Model 85 has a 10-

round detachable box magazine. Among other specialized optics, these rifles can be equipped with the L1 Starlight scope.

FR-F2

This bolt-action 7.62mm NATO sniper's rifle is based on the MAS-36 and has a 10-round magazine. The butt stock is adjustable for length through extension pieces. It also has a pistol grip, folding bipod, and flash suppressor. Unlike many of the other sniper's rifles used by HRUs, the FR-F2 is relatively light at a little over 8 pounds. The standard telescopic sight is a 6x42mm with a range drum marked up to 800 meters and a reticle illumination system. The Sopelem OB50 image intensifier can be fitted for night usage.

FN Sniper

This 7.62mm NATO bolt action uses a Mauser action and has a 5-round magazine. Its heavy barrel, which is fitted with a flash suppressor, at 19.7 inches is relatively short for a sniping rifle. It weighs about 11 1/2 pounds and can be used with or without a bipod.

Tikka Finlander Model 55

This heavy barreled bolt action is intended primarily as a close-range (urban) sniping rifle. In .22/250 caliber, it is capable of better than one minute of angle. It has a free-floating barrel in a wooden stock with a pistol grip. Detachable magazines in 3-, 5-, and 10-round capacities are available. The weapon is also available in .243 Winchester and 7.62mm NATO caliber.

M21

This is the sniper's version of the U.S. M-14 rifle. Chambered for the 7.62mm NATO round, this semi-automatic rifle is constructed of specially selected and tuned components and then fitted with a Leatherwood variable telescopic sight. This rifle is highly accurate and is well capable of better than one minute of angle.

S-S SR

This special-purpose sniper's rifle is silenced ("suppressed") for HRU/special operations uses. It uses a Sako bolt action chambered for a subsonic 7.62mm NATO round. The Vaime silencer is 660mm long and encloses the barrel completely.

ASSAULT RIFLES AND SHOTGUNS

Although the handgun, submachine gun, and sniper's rifle are the three primary weapons of HRUs, most units have assault rifles and shotguns in their arsenals as well. In some cases, a compact assault rifle such as the Steyr AUG or CAR-15 is used as a cross between a SMG and assault rifle. Normally, however, this is a poor compromise since the short assault rifles still fire 5.56mm rounds, which will overpenetrate when used on airplanes, ships, or buildings. Assault rifles do have a valid place in the HRU's armory, but not as the principal weapon for an assault team. Other assault rifles which have received substantial use among HRUs are the M-16, FN-FAL, Galil, G3, and AK-47.

Even in the hands of a very skilled user, the fighting shotgun is not selective enough to be used as a primary assault weapon. For many HRUs, its primary purpose is for shooting the hinges or locks off doors during a forced entry. The shotgun can also be used in certain assault situations where hostages are not present or in roadblock situations.

Short-barreled, 12-gauge slide-action or automatic shotguns are the standard for HRU usage. Overwhelmingly, the Remington 870 is the most popular choice. Others which have received some usage are the Ithaca

37 and Winchester Defender, both of which are slide actions. Normally, the 18- to 20-inch barrel is chosen for HRU usage, though some units use even shorter barrels for close-range work. Other shotguns worthy of note for HRU usage include the SPAS-12, which is a semiauto that can also be used as a slide action, and the Benelli Police/Military which I rate as the best assault shotgun in the world.

SPECIAL OPTICS AND
SIGHTING DEVICES

Since the power will often be cut during an HRU's assault and/or the area will frequently be obscured with smoke, various types of low-light or fast-acquisition optics are desirable for HRU weapons. Snipers may also have to take a precision shot in poor light; hence, the variety of special optics available for the sniper's rifle. When one considers the incredible confusion which may reign during an assault amidst the smoke from stun or gas grenades, the screams of hostages, and the firing of friend and foe, a device which aids in rapid target acquisition can be invaluable. Likewise, since an HRU sniper may have to acquire a target and fire in an instant, often in poor light, special optics may literally be a matter of life or death.

For use on assault weapons, various laser-aiming devices are quite useful. These devices are mounted on the weapon and, when turned on, place a red dot on a target at the point where a bullet will strike. Obviously, this is a real aid to rapid-target acquisition in low light. Except in very bright light conditions, the laser spot can be seen out to ranges of 100 yards or greater. However, it must be borne in mind that the laser does not illuminate the target—it only marks it. Various types of laser sights can be mounted on pistols, SMGs, shotguns, assault rifles, or sniper's rifles. Among the companies making effective laser-aiming devices are Laser Products, Soginco, and Lasergage.

Other types of light intensifiers may be mounted on weapons, normally the SMG or assault or sniper's rifle. Usually, such units consist of an image intensifier and a power source in a self-contained unit. Such devices are often referred to as *first generation* or *second generation*. In both cases, the unit takes the light that is available and intensifies it so that visibility is enhanced thousands of times. Since such units rely on available light, they are known as passive intensifiers. In simple terms, first-generation devices do not offer quite as distortion-free an image as second-generation devices, though the latter may not have the resolution of the former. Second-generation devices tend to be more compact. To confuse matters even more, *third-generation* devices, which can operate with virtually no available light, exist as well, but they are very expensive.

The above explanation is, of course, grossly simplistic.

Night-vision rifle scopes can grant one inch accuracy at 200 meters in starlight, which should give a simple illustration of why they are in the inventory of virtually every major HRU. Some of the more sophisticated night-vision scopes can even detect other night-vision devices. The light gain yielded by a night-vision image-intensifying scope can be up to 80,000 times. Among the companies offering such devices are Security Research International, Bonaventure, Javelin, Smith & Wesson, Litton Industries, Eltro, Hensold, and various others.

Infrared Nite-Site

Another type of night-vision device which is in use with some HRUs is the infrared Nite-Site, which includes a lamp that produces an infrared beam and a viewer to sight on objects so illuminated.

These nite sites tend to be bulky and would normally only be mounted on a sniper's rifle. Because they supply their own infrared light, such scopes are known as "active" night-vision devices. Since fog or smoke can reflect the beam, infrared devices do not work well during an assault when gas or smoke grenades are used. Among those companies offering infrared devices are Nite Hawk, Inc. and Eltro.

Selected Armson Products

Still another device which has the advantage of being very compact is the Armson O.E.G. (Occluded Eye Sight) which superimposes a red dot on the target. It is meant to be used with both eyes open and works with the user's night vision to allow rapid target acquisition. Armson also offers a special telescopic sight to certain HRUs which uses crosshairs. A third item from Armson in use with some HRUs is Tritium pistol and SMG sights which use dots in the front and rear sights that glow in the dark and allow rapid sight alignment in low light.

Other Products

Somewhat similar to the Armson O.E.G. is the Aimpoint Electronic Sight which also uses an illuminated red dot. One final device to be mentioned in this category is the "Blind Pugh," which projects a black spot on the target. This is an especially effective device for close-range use in blackout conditions.

Because of its wide use by HRUs, an especially large variety of night-vision devices is available for the H&K MP5. The H&K Aiming Projector, though complicated, in fact, set a standard for other specialized optics.

SPECIAL-PURPOSE AMMUNITION

Various ammunition manufacturers produce special ammunition designed to enhance the capabilities of HRU weapons for certain situations. Normally, when an HRU member needs to shoot he must deliver instant stopping power to the target to keep him from harming the hostages. The perfect example of the need for proper ammunition occurred during the GSG-9 assault at Mogadishu when the .38 Special loads carried by the assault team failed to instantly stop the terrorist leader, allowing him to throw a grenade.

For handguns, submachine guns, and rifles, the Glaser Safety Slug is particularly noteworthy and particularly deadly. The Glaser, which is filled with small #2 shot sealed with Teflon into a copper case, is designed to penetrate harder mediums (such as wood) and then fragment to deliver devastating power against flesh. A special advantage of the Glaser for HRUs is that despite its devastating killing power, it does not present much danger from ricochets to bystanders or members of an assault force. Among the calibers for which Glasers are available are .25 ACP, .32 ACP, .380 ACP, 9x19mm, .38 Super ACP, .38 Special, .357 Magnum, .44 Special, .44 Magnum, .45 ACP, .45 Colt, 7.62mm NATO, and .30-06. When used by an HRU sniper, the two rifle rounds will literally destroy a head or chest.

For use against terrorists who are wearing body armor or are situated behind some type of barrier, the KTW armor-piercing round is very useful. The KTW bullet is designed for very high velocity and is of a bronze alloy covered with Teflon. The three primary handgun calibers used by HRUs (9mm, .38 Special, and .357 Magnum) and the primary SMG caliber (9mm) are available in KTW. Note that in normal hostage situations, the KTW round would overpenetrate.

Another high-velocity bullet which delivers a lot of hydrostatic shock is the French THV load in .357 Magnum or 9mm. The German BAT round offers good expansion, too, yet feeds reliably in automatic weapons due to a thin copper cap which fits in the bullet's hollow cavity. Once again, the 9mm and .357 Magnum BAT rounds will probably be of most interest to the HRU.

For those units using such weapons as the CAR-15 or Steyr AUG in the assault role, special expanding ammo, such as the Federal "blitz" round, is available so that overpenetration and danger from ricochets are reduced. Light loads of various types are also available for use in suppressed weapons. In some loadings for suppressed 9mm weapons, a heavier bullet is used at lower velocity, thereby retaining the knockdown power.

Special shotgun rounds designed for HRUs should be mentioned as well. The Ferret, for example, is a barricade-penetrating 12-gauge round which will deliver CS or CN gas. Another special shotgun round, known as the Shok-Lok, is designed to blow hinges or locks off doors or shutters more effectively than the normal buckshot or slug load.

There are other types of munitions available to HRUs, some of which are classified as to their characteristics. In many cases, the demand for some of the more esoteric rounds is so limited that they are produced on a very limited scale. Even regular ammunition used by HRUs is often subjected to special production and quality-control procedures. The Norma .357 Magnum ammo fabricated for GIGN, for example, is manufactured on a special production line with more intensive quality-control procedures and special waterproofing techniques.

EQUIPMENT

In addition to weapons, other types of devices are critical to an HRU so that it can acquire intelligence, communicate, protect the operator, gain entry to the objective, create diversions, carry out a search and clearance, and carry out various other tasks.

Intelligence-Gathering and Surveillance Devices

The HRU faces the rather difficult task of gathering

intelligence concerning all aspects of its objective without the terrorists realizing that they are under close observation (otherwise, the terrorists would be tipped off about the possibility of an assault). Various types of specialized night-vision devices similar to those mounted on weapons can also be used to gather intelligence. Like telescopic sights, these devices can be either passive or active. When used for surveillance, starlight or infrared observation devices can be more bulky than those mounted on weapons and, consequently, perhaps gain in effectiveness. The sniper, of course, contributes a great deal of intelligence using the optics mounted on his weapon.

Other types of visual devices are also used in gathering intelligence as well. Closed-circuit television cameras, for example, may be used if they can be emplaced clandestinely. Thermal imaging systems may also be useful in certain, but very limited, applications. Thermal imagers, however, are prey to many disadvantages; glass windows, for one, can defeat them. It takes great skill and constant temperature conditions for a thermal imaging operator to even judge whether or not a subject has moved from one room to another.

If it can be emplaced, perhaps the most effective device available is the endoscope, a fibre-optic pinhole lens developed primarily for medical and industrial applications. Such lenses offer a wide angle view of a room through the tiniest pinhole in a wall. The problem is, of course, getting the pinhole drilled without being detected. As a result, drills which can be used ultra-quietly are prized by HRUs. If they can be emplaced, closed-circuit television cameras are useful, too.

Intelligence may also be gained through an array of sophisticated listening devices. Electronic stethoscopes may be used for listening through walls to detect sounds in an adjacent room. Directional microphones may also be used in situations where subjects are in the open. Some units have laser infrarometers which theoretically can pick up speech from vibrations caused on windows or other objects in the room. So far, however, such devices have not been very effective.

The most effective audio device so far is, in fact, a sensitive microphone or transmitter emplaced by dangling it down a chimney or, in subminiature form, smuggling it into the target area.

Two instances of extremely effective use of surveillance devices occurred at Princes Gate and at Train 747 where the SAS and the Royal Dutch Marines managed to determine the locations of the terrorists and hostages rather effectively using surveillance devices. On the other hand, one of the reasons the Egyptian assault on the hijacked airliner on Malta was such an abysmal failure was the failure to make an attempt to use technology to determine the whereabouts of the terrorists.

COMMUNICATIONS

The radio transceiver used by HRU members must possess three primary characteristics: it must be compact, operate in hands-off fashion, and offer a secure net. It must also be highly reliable, since communications (commo) is critical during an assault using various elements. Normally, UHF bands are necessary to provide communications security. Some radios can actually be built into ballistic helmets for HRU purposes. Trunking technology allows communications between all members of a team and the unit commander during an operation. Trunked systems, it should be mentioned, are hard to monitor, thus enhancing security. Various special-purpose commo equipment is available, as well. For example, the Tadiran PRC-601 Transceiver is designed for use by combat swimmers and can be used underwater. Communication technology changes so frequently that any specific systems discussed will likely be outdated quickly, but three examples of viable HRU radio systems are: the PVS 5400 or PVS 5500, the MX300, and the ASR3.

An especially important use of communications often

occurs when snipers must deal with multiple targets simultaneously (as at Djibouti). Although there is a device which will automatically fire a group of rifles simultaneously on command, I am not in favor of its use, preferring that the sniper himself pull the trigger.)

Body Armor and Assault Vests

Although the HRU relies on speed and surprise during an assault, the possibility still exists for terrorists to get off shots at members of the assault force. As a result, virtually all HRUs use some type of ballistic vest to protect the vital areas and may use some form of ballistic helmet. To carry the equipment necessary for infiltration and assault, many HRUs employ specialized vests as well.

Ballistic Helmets. Although balaclavas or berets may be impressive and anti-flash hoods may be practical, none of this headgear will stop a bullet. As a result, many HRUs employ some type of ballistic helmet to protect the face and skull. Polycarbonate is probably the most common material from which such helmets and face masks are fabricated. Most of these helmets are designed so that a gas mask can be worn with them. Many of the ballistic helmets in use will stop a .357 Magnum bullet fired from as close as three meters. Of course, any helmet chosen must not be so heavy or bulky that it inhibits mobility of members of the assault force. One reason some units do not use ballistic helmets is that they find they substantially slow down the acquisition of a target.

Two units in particular which assault in ballistic helmets are GSG-9 and NOCS, though there are others. An added advantage of such helmets, especially when fitted with a visor, is that they help prevent the dust, grit, and other debris thrown up by a stun grenade from getting into the eyes and obscuring the vision as one rapidly follows the grenade in. Personally, although I like the protection given by ballistic helmets, I find that they

inhibit my ability to rapidly acquire targets and sometimes get in the way during a silent pre-assault approach.

Ballistic Vests. Although soft body armor employing
layers of Kevlar has become standard for everyday wear
by many police forces and some HRUs providing VIP
protection, the assault team needs heavier duty assault
vests with ceramic inserts in addition to Kevlar layers.
As with helmets, however, the assault vest represents
a trade-off between maneuverability and protection.
Such "tactical" vests with inserts will often stop up to
a .30-06 bullet. The most effective of such armor will
normally protect the front and back of the torso, over
the shoulders, the neck, sides, and groin. Some vests
combine ballistic protection with additional external
pockets for spare ammunition, stun grenades, radios,
and other equipment, thereby functioning as a combination ballistic vest/load-carrying assault vest.

Among the companies which supply ballistic armor
to HRUs are Bristol (one of the most widely used,
probably because of its employment by the SAS and
GSG-9), especially the grade 64 and grade 86; FN;
Berka IWKA, which are very light for the protection
offered; Hagar; Armor of America; Burlington; and
Second Chance, especially the Command Jac and Hard
Corps.

Second Chance keeps track of the number of police
officers who have been saved by wearing one of their
vests—normally one of the "soft" under-uniform vests—
and the number runs into the three hundreds or more.
One particular case involving a Bristol vest which I
recall involved a European HRU member who took two
.32 ACP rounds in his vest as he jumped in front of a
hostage, yet he still managed to kill the assailant with
return fire. The HRU member was barely bruised by the
two hits his vest took.

Normally when one thinks of "armor" for HRUs,
one thinks of ballistic protection. Due to the movement
(including rappelling, scaling, and rapid entry) often
required during an assault and the likelihood of bump-

ing into doorways and window sills, the HRU member also needs protection from injury to the elbows, knees, and other exposed body parts. A friend of mine who trains police entry teams recently made an interesting suggestion in regard to this problem. There is special underwear with built-in padding designed for Motorcross racers. This underwear lends itself well to HRU usage. The SAS and some other units build padding into the elbows and knees of their assault suits as well.

Load-Carrying Assault Vests. Load-carrying assault vests are designed to carry equipment such as radios, stun or gas grenades, pistols, spare ammo, first aid kit, and knife. Frequently, a rappelling harness is built into the vest. Many such vests incorporate Kevlar layers, thereby also functioning as ballistic vests. It should be noted that the proper placement of spare magazines about the vest, in effect, increases its ballistic efficiency as well. Among the better load-carrying vests (available from Combat Equipment Sales) is one which has a rappelling harness built in; it does not, however, provide ballistic protection. Elevated Urban Operations also offers a very useful vest in their SOV (Special Operations Vest).

Breaching and Entry Devices. Within this category fall such mundane items as rappelling ropes and such sophisticated devices as high-speed cutting torches. For descent, abseiling, rappelling—whatever term is used—three basic components are normally needed: a well-designed rope (such as that offered by Marlow Rope Company), a descendeur (which can be of various types and may include a dead man's stop or some other sophisticated control device), and the harness. Descendeurs are becoming increasingly more sophisticated and include such devices as the Rollgliss locking-brake system, which can be controlled with one hand during a descent while the other hand keeps the pistol or SMG at the ready. The Inter Risk Abseil 3 Speed Descendeur offers all sorts of special features: it is hand-held for normal descent; brakes automatically when released;

has slow, medium, and rapid descent speeds; and allows both hands free for shooting while static. One other sophisticated descendeur is the IKAR/AS1 (which will allow a rapid descent at up to 5.5 meters per second). IKAR also makes what many consider to be the best rappelling harness for HRUs, one which offers security and comfort during the descent.

Even with good equipment and highly trained personnel, problems can still occur. Remember that at Princes Gate, an SAS man descending the rear face of the Iranian embassy became entangled and could not complete his descent.

The rappelling rig allows members of the HRU to descend to assault, but they may also have to ascend; therefore, certain devices are available for tactical ascents as well. Also extremely useful are ladders. Special assault ladders are normally light in weight (often due to their aluminum construction) and designed for silent employment through the use of pads. I.R. Management, Ltd., has developed a special line of assault ladders designed with strength, lightness, and quietness in mind. Many are designed with special hooks at the top, while others may be used for bridging or as a sniper's platform. Along with ladders, the really sophisticated HRUs have a comprehensive spec book telling them exactly what lengths of ladders are needed to reach the wings or doors of various types of aircraft, or specs relating to other likely targets. After all, it may not be possible to measure prior to an assault!

More esoteric ascent equipment includes climbing aids which may be affixed to the boots and grapnels and ropes. CDME has a special air cannon, in fact, for launching grapnels quietly.

For gaining entry by breaching, various devices are available as well. Some are as simple as sledgehammers or bolt cutters, while others are rather sophisticated. At Princes Gate, for example, sledgehammers proved invaluable when the frame charges could not be used to blow windows in the rear of the embassy.

For explosive entry, various types of charges must be in the HRU's inventory. LINEX, for example, is especially useful since it is flexible and can be bent in 90-degree angles for emplacement. Other types of prefabricated charges can be used as frame charges or in constructing water impulse, terminal, or other types of explosive entry devices.

Special-purpose devices, such as the Entacannon, may also be used. The Entacannon is an air-powered device which uses a projectile to breach brick walls or doors. For cutting through steel doors and barred windows, the HRU must also have thermal cutting torches available. The Arcair Slice Pak and the CDME Thermal Arc Shoulder Pak are two such devices which are portable and effective enough to serve HRUs.

Diversionary Device. The primary diversionary device is the stun grenade, which was designed to provide a blinding flash and a loud report without producing fragmentation which might be lethal. The effect of the stun grenade is disorientation on the part of the terrorist so that he freezes and/or ducks. (It is hoped that the stun grenade will also force the hostages to keep their heads down.)

It is imperative, however, that the assault team follow the stun grenade in quickly. This was graphically illustrated when D11 hesitated after throwing its stun grenades when trying to break a hostage situation in Northolt, Middlesex, and the hostage-taker had time to repeatedly stab a hostage.

Stun grenades are available in single or multiple-bang versions. I have been inside a room acting as a "hostage" during exercises in which stun grenades exploded less than five feet from me and though the 2,000,000+ candle power and 200+ decibels certainly did disorient me—even though I knew they were coming—I can attest that there was no permanent damage. The primary disadvantages of the stun grenade have been smoke (which may obscure the assault team's vision) and the possibility of fire. There are various producers of stun grenades, including NICO-Pyrotechnik, Schermuly, Accuracy Systems, and INCO (which produces a "blinding grenade" which relies solely on flash and which is so bright that it does take a few days for vision to return to normal).

Stun grenades, it should be remembered, played an important role in two of the five rescues I consider classics (Mogadishu and Princes Gate). Stun grenades have also been used successfully on numerous other occasions. As far as I know, the only instance where a stun grenade proved fatal was in a situation where a suspect in, I believe, a narcotics raid somehow ended up with a stun grenade pressed between her back and a wall when it went off.

Another diversionary device sometimes encountered is the strobe gun produced by Security Equipment Supplies. The strobe gun produces no lasting effect, either, but it does have a disorienting effect to a greater or lesser extent, causing a subject to turn away (at the minimum).

* * *

By no means should the above listing be considered a comprehensive survey of HRU equipment. It is intended only to offer an overview of the types of devices available to help the HRU accomplish its mission. To aid in the war against terrorism, HRUs are constantly upgrading their technological capabilities to gain every edge possible to successfully accomplish their mission.

Opposite: Remington Model 870 is shown with Laser Sight integrated into the weapon (top) and with Laser Products Target Illumination System installed (center).

At bottom is the H&K MP5SDA2, the suppressed, fixed stock version of this HRU standby.

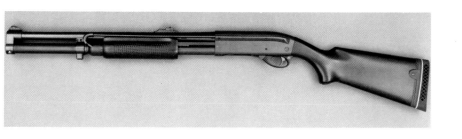

The H&K MP5SD3, the suppressed version with telescoping stock, is shown (top). The effective Laser Sight, a Laser Products device, is shown above mounted on an H&K MP5 carbine.

After the H&K MP5 system, the Uzi is the most widely used SMG among HRUs. The Mini Uzi is shown at the top of the photograph below, while the standard Uzi is pictured beneath it.

St. Augustin 2, den 21. 11. 1977

... freundliche ... und ehre...
... se ... haben,
wir uns ... gefre... rer Bevölkerung hat uns
so großer Teile ...
Damit hatten wir nicht gerechnet.
hat nur ihre Pflicht erfüllt !

t herzlichen Grüßen

(W e g e n e r)
Kommandeur der GSG 9

19330   HK INC ARL VA 22201
19330   IB

The H&K P7 9mm auto (opposite), used by GSG-9 and a few other HRUs, has the advantage o being very compact for a 9mm auto and is ready for instant use due to its squeeze-cockin device.

The Steyr AUG 5.56mm assault rifle (below) has begun to achieve popularity with HRU though it isn't really well suited for most assault situations as is the SMG.

The French FR-F2 sniper's rifle (bottom) is used by GIGN and a few other HRUs.

The AR-15 is pictured with the Target Illumination System from Laser Products.

Although not as widely used as the H&K MP5, the Beretta M12 still sees substantial use with HRUs.

Beretta Model 92F with Model 312 Target Illumination System installed.

Colt Government Model with Laser Products' Model 310 Target Illumination System installed is shown above. This system can be slipped on or off in a matter of minutes. Such a light would be most useful for an assault team's point man.

By far the most popular handgun in the world for HRU use is the Browning Hi-Power, shown at right. Its popularity stems, in part, from its use by the Special Air Service.

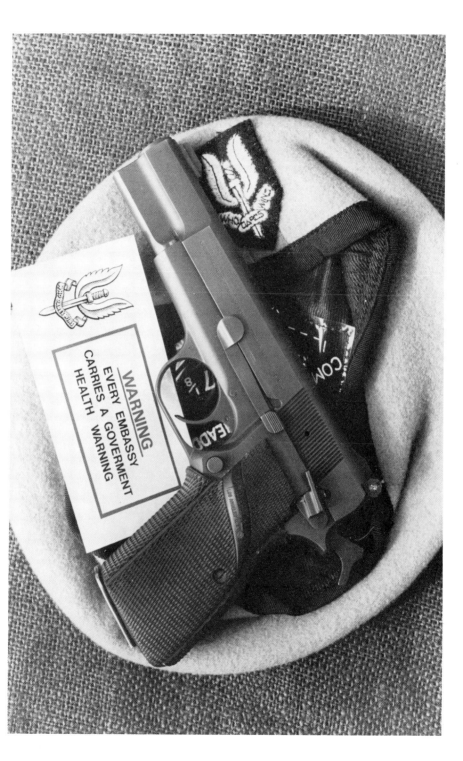

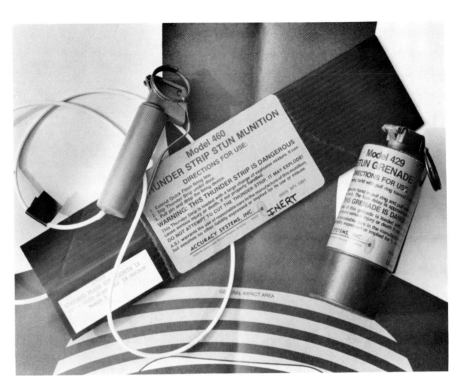

A "Thunder Strip," which can be slid under a door and detonated in order to disorient those within, is shown at left, with "flash bang" stun grenade next to it.

Arcair Cutpacks, below, are widely used by HRUs to cut through steel doors and bars. From left to right: Slice Pak Basic, Slice Pak Complete, and Slice Pak Battery Unit. Photo courtesy of Arcair Company.

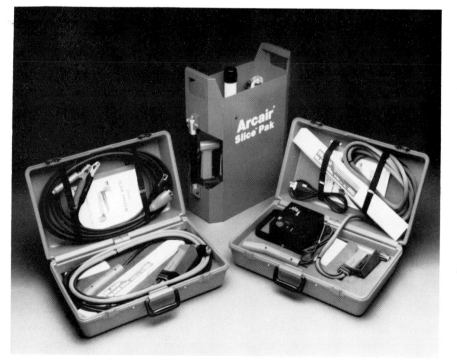

A member of GIGN is pictured practicing with the Manurhin .357 Magnum revolver. In addition to two-handed shooting, the GIGN does a lot of one-handed shooting as well.

Clockwise from top left: Insignia of the Sultan of Oman's Special Force (note the SAS influence on the wings); proposed insignia for the FBI HRT which was vetoed by an FBI official because there were no "elite" units within the FBI needing their own insignia; insignia of the Spanish UEI; insignia of the Sudanese HRU, the 144th Parachute battalion; breast qualification badge worn by members of the Portuguese GEO; GIGN insignia (the left one is normally worn on the jacket but is worn as a pocket crest when metal; the right one is worn on diving suits); insignia worn by the Honduran COE.

Clockwise from top left: Spanish GEO insignia; new GSG-9 pocket badge bearing a RamAir parachute to illustrate the unit's parachute skills; original GSG-9 pocket badge; breast badges worn by the Venezuelan HRU; original insignia worn by the Tunisian GCGN is shown at left, and the current insignia at right; insignia of the Egyptian Unit 777; insignia of ESI, the Belgian national HRU. The Belgian insignia bears the unit's name in Flemish (top) and French (bottom) since both are official languages. Depicted is the goddess Diana, the unit's code name/call sign.

APPENDIX II

HRU Units and Terms

AVESCOM. Philippine Aviations Security Commando, which provides an anti-hijacking HRU.

Balaclava. Knitted hood worn by some HRU members to hide the face and act as camouflage.

Beredskapstrop. Readiness Troop, Norwegian National Police HRU.

Blue Light. Interim U.S. anti-terrorist unit formed at Fort Bragg to act as a national HRU until Delta was fully trained.

Body armor. Ballistic protection worn by HRU assault units, frequently referred to as a "bulletproof vest."

Breaching. Gaining entry to an area where hostages are held, frequently with explosives but possibly by other methods.

Cobras Political Squadron. HRU of the Honduran Public Security Forces.

Cobra Unit. Austrian HRU officially known as the *Gendarmerieeinsatz kommando* (Gendarmerie Special Unit).

COE (Comando de Operaciones Especiales). HRU of the Honduran Special Forces Command.

Comacchio Company. Special British Royal Marine Commando Unit with anti-terrorist responsibility for the North Sea oil fields.

CQB (Close Quarters Battle). Techniques of close-range combat with pistol, submachine gun, shotguns, knives, and unarmed.

DEA (Dimoria Eidikon Apostolon). The Special Mission Platoon of the Athens City Police, which acts as the major Greek HRU.

D11. London Metropolitan Police containment and hostage rescue unit drawn from police firearms instructors.

Delta. U.S. Army anti-terrorist unit, formed primarily of Special Forces personnel.

Detachment 81. Special Commando Team of the Indonesian Army Special Forces.

Emergency Response Teams. HRUs of the Royal Canadian Mounted Police.

Endoscope. A fibre-optic, pin-hole lens which can give a wide-angle view into a room through a tiny opening. Used by HRUs for surveillance and intelligence gathering.

EOD. Explosive Ordnance Disposal Unit.

ESI (Escadron Special d'Intervention). Belgian HRU of the Gendarmerie Royale.

FACH. Chilean Air Force anti-hijacking unit.

Fast roping. Rapid insertion method akin to rappelling, to allow HRU members to rapidly slide down a rope from a helicopter.

Force 777. Current Egyptian HRU under the Army Commandos.

Fromandskorpset. Danish combat swimmers who provide anti-terrorist capability for ports, oil rigs, etc.

GAES. Anti-extortion and anti-kidnapping groups of the Colombian Army.

GAJDA. Anti-hijacking units of the Colombian Air Force.

Garda Siochana. Irish National Police, the Special Branch of which provides the national HRU.

General Staff Recon Unit. Israeli HRU which comes directly under the IDF general staff.

GEO (Grupo Especial de Operaciones). HRU of the Spanish Policia Nacional.

GEOS. Special Operations Group of the Colombian Policia Nacional.

GIGN (Groupement D'Intervention De La Gendarmerie Nationale). French national HRU drawn from the militarized Gendarmerie. Morocco also has an HRU of the same name.

GIS (Groupe Interventional Speciale). HRU of the Italian Carabinieri.

GOPE (Grupo de Operaciones Especiales). HRU of the Chilean Caribineros.

Groupement de Commando of the Garde Nationale. HRU of the Tunisian Gendarmerie.

Grupo de Operacoes Especiais. Portuguese HRU of the Policia de Seguranca Publica.

GSG-9 (Grenzschutzgruppe 9). German HRU within the Federal Border Police.

GSU. General Services Unit of the Kenya Police, the Recce Unit of which provides the national HRU.

Halcon 8. Argentinian Special Counter-Terrorism Team of the Army Commandos.

HRT. The "Hurt" or Hostage Response Team of the FBI, the U.S. national HRU for internal terrorist incidents.

HRU (Hostage Rescue Unit). The most widely used term to describe anti-terrorist or anti-hijacking units.

Killing House. Special room or group of rooms designed for practicing assault tactics and combat shooting. This term comes from the British SAS.

Komissar. West German computer system to keep track of terrorists.

Light intensifier. Device to allow the HRU member to see in very low-light conditions by enhancing any light available thousands of times.

LRF (Light Reaction Forces). HRU of the Philippine Constabulary.

Mossad. Israeli Intelligence Agency.

Moukafaha. Lebanese Army HRU.

NEST (Nuclear Emergency Search Teams). Special technical unit within the Department of Energy to deal with a terrorist threat involving nuclear materials.

NOCS (Nucleo Operativo Centrale di Sicurezza). Italian HRU which rescued U.S. Brigadier General Dozier.

101st Special Forces Battalion. Jordanian unit which provides the national HRU.

144th CTU (Counter Terrorist Unit). Sudanese HRU.

Osasto Karhu. Also known as the "Bear Unit." The Finnish HRU of the Helsinki Mobile Police.

OSS (Office of Strategic Services). World War II U.S. intelligence and sabotage unit which evolved into the CIA and the Special Forces.

Ozel Intihar Kommando Boluga. The Jandara Suicide Commandos, the Turkish HRU.

PET (Politiets Efterretningstjeneste). Danish State Police Intelligence Service HRU.

Police Special Action Units. Japanese police HRUs.

Police Special Task Force. South African HRU under the Security Branch of the police.

Police Tactical Team. Singapore Police HRU.

Projecto Talon. HRU of the Brazilian Army Special Forces.

Puma Unit. HRU of the Ecuadorian Army.

Rappelling. Method of rapidly lowering assault team members or snipers into position on structures or natural heights.

Saiqa. "Lightning." The original Egyptian Army HRU which carried out the abortive aircraft assault on Cyprus in 1978.

SAS (Special Air Service). British elite raiding and counterinsurgency unit, which also provides the British HRU. Both Australia and New Zealand also have SAS units which provide HRUs.

Sayaret Matkal. Israeli HRU/anti-terrorist unit.

SBS (Special Boat Squadron). Combat swimmer unit of the British Royal Marine Commandos, which has certain anti-terrorist duties, including North Sea oil rig security.

SEAL Team 6. U.S. Navy combat swimmer unit trained for anti-terrorist missions and assigned to Delta.

SEK (Speziale-insatz Kommando). German police equivalent of a U.S. SWAT Team.

SOE (Special Operations Executive). British unit formed in World War II to carry out sabotage in occupied countries.

Son Tay Raid. Raid by U.S. Special Forces into North Vietnam to rescue American POWs.

SOP (Standard Operating Procedure). The established procedure for dealing with certain situations.

Special Security Force. Saudi Arabian HRU.

Stockholm Syndrome. The team used to describe the

psychological tendency hostages have to develop empathy with their captors.

Stun grenades. Devices which through a bright flash and loud report disorient terrorists during an assault without permanently injuring any hostages present in the room.

Sultan's Special Force. HRU of the Omani Special Forces.

Suppressed weapon. Accepted term for weapons employing a noise-suppression device; what are generally known as "silenced" weapons.

SWAT. Special Weapons and Tactics Teams, normally within police forces, trained to deal with domestic or criminal hostage situations and more fully equipped than normal police personnel.

Thermal imager. Device which can be used to track the location of living things due to heat differentials between their body heat and the surrounding environment. Though used by many HRUs, the thermal imager is prey to many variables.

UAT (Unidad Anti-Terrorista). Combined Army/ Police Chilean HRU.

UEI (Unidad Especial de Intervencion). HRU of the Spanish Guardia Civil.

U-Group. Bahrain HRU of the Public Security Force.

Unit Timpaan Khas. Special Strike Unit of the Royal Malaysian Police, which provides that country's HRU.

APPENDIX III

Terrorist Groups, A Glossary

To understand the magnitude and complexity of the terrorist threat, one must understand the large number of terrorist groups which have come into existence during the last two decades. Though their political aims may vary widely, all share the basic philosophy that violence is an acceptable means to their ends. The following list is by no means complete and will have already become at least slightly dated by the time this book is published since new terrorist groups are constantly incubating. Still, the terrorist guide to terrorist groups active during the last quarter of a century covers most of those which have caused the need for the national anti-terrorist units which are the subject of this work.

AKO (Anarchistische Kampforganization). Swiss anarchist group most active during the 1970s.

Al Fatah. Palestinian group closely affiliated with Black September.

Al Zulfiqah. Pakistani group opposed to President Zeia.

ALN. Brazilian Action for National Liberation.

ARC. French group.

Armenian Secret Army of Liberation. Terrorist group which seeks to take revenge on the Turks for past atrocities against Armenians.

Baader Meinhof Gang. Alternate name for the West German RAF based on the names of two founders—Andreas Baader and Ulrike Meinhof. Also see RAF.

Black June Organization. Radical Palestinian group.

Black September. Radical Palestinian group responsible for hijackings and the Munich massacre. Name was taken from the month in which King Hussein turned the Arab Legion loose on the Palestinians in Jordan.

Breton Liberation Front. Marxist separatist movement in France, also known in French as FLB *(Front de Liberation de La Bretogne)* or ARB *(Armee Revolutionnaire Bretonne).* Has known links with the IRA.

CCC. Belgian Fighting Communist Cells. One of the recent anti-NATO groups which is probably KGB controlled.

Croatian Revolutionary Brotherhood. Also known as HRB *(Hrvatsko Revolucionarno Bratstvo).* It has carried out bombings and hijackings against the Yugoslav government because of its domination by Serbs.

Dev-Sol. Left-wing Turkish revolutionary organization.

Direct Action. Formed by merging the NAPAP and French Red Brigades, this French group is involved with other anti-NATO groups. Carlos is known to have been involved with this group.

Dutch Red Help. Left-wing group which trained with the Palestinians and has also carried out courier and other duties for the Palestinians. It has given assistance to the IRA.

ELN. Bolivian terrorist/"liberation" movement.

EOKA (Ethniki Organosis Kypriakou Agonistov). Cypriot terrorist group.

ERP. Left-wing Argentine group which in the 1970s worked with the Tupamaros and other left-wing groups in Latin America.

ETA (Euzakadi Ta Askatasuma). Basque separatist movement which has carried out sabotage, assassination, and kidnapping, including the murder of Spanish Prime Minister Carrero Blanco. Although most ETA operations have been carried out in Spain, a few have spilled over into France.

FALN (Fuerzos Armados de la Liberacion Nacional). Puerto Rican terrorist group which has carried out numerous bombings on the mainland and which in 1981 was plotting to kidnap President Reagan's son.

FAR. Armed Revolutionary Force, Cuban-backed Guatemalan group which assassinated the American ambassador to that country in 1968.

FLN. Algerian National Liberation Front. Active during the late French Colonial Period in Algeria.

FLO. Quebec liberation group responsible for bombings and assassinations.

FP-25. Portuguese anti-NATO group.

FRAP. Leninist Spanish Group.

French Red Brigades. Copy of the Italian Red Brigades but nowhere near as numerous—nor as effective.

Frepalina. Paraguayan National Liberation Front. Part of the *Junta de Co-ordinacion Revolucionaria* formed of various South American terrorist groups.

GAP. Italian group which trained commandos in the Peidmont Mountains and with the Palestinians.

Gauche Proletariene. French group.

German Revolutionary Cells. West German group.

GRAPO (Grupo de Resistencia Antifascista Primo de Octubre). Leftist Spanish group which has carried out kidnappings, bombings, assassinations, and bank robberies, including the assassination of four policemen on 1 October 1975 in retaliation for the execution of five urban guerrillas.

Grey Wolves. Right-wing Turkish terrorist group, the militant arm of the National Action Party.

Guerrilleros Del Cristo Rey. Warriors of Christ the King. Right-wing Spanish neo-Nazi group.

INLA (Irish National Liberation Army). Even more militant than the IRA.

IRA (Irish Republican Army). Long-standing Irish

nationalist group fighting to unite Ireland. Also see PIRA.

Islamic Jihad. Shi'ite terrorist group responsible for the bombing of the U.S. embassy and Marine compound in Beirut and probably the largest single terrorist threat to the USA. Descended from the Medieval Assassins cult.

Italian Front for the Liberation of the Proletariat. Anti-NATO Italian group.

JCAG (Justice Commandos of Armenian Genocide). Group which has carried out assassinations of Turkish diplomats worldwide, including in the United States.

JDL (Jewish Defense League). U.S. militant Jewish group which has carried out terrorist attacks against perceived enemies of Jews, most active in New York City.

JRA (Japanese Red Army). Also known as Sekigun. Japanese terrorist group formed in 1969. Carried out various kidnappings, embassy seizures, and hijackings, but it is best known for the massacre of 26 people at Lod Airport in support of the PFLP. The JRA has proved very useful to the PFLP since its members obviously don't look like Palestinians.

JRC (Junta for Revolutionary Coordination). Multinational Latin American group formed by the Tupamaros.

KAWA Group. Kurdish nationalist group trained by Palestinians; primarily anti-Turkish and part of the TPLA.

Kommando Jihid. Islamic fundamentalist terrorist group

which hijacked an Indonesian airliner to Thailand in 1981.

Lebanese Armed Revolutionary Faction. One of the many and varied Lebanese terrorist groups. Responsible for assassinating Americans.

MAR (Movimiento de Accion Revolcionaria). Mexican terrorist group funded by the KGB.

MIR. Chilean terrorist group.

Montoneros. Left-wing pro-Peron Argentinian group which has carried out assassinations, kidnappings, and bombings. Most active during the mid-1970s.

M19. Colombian terrorist group heavily involved in kidnapping and drugs to raise money.

Moro National Liberation Front. Radical Philippine terrorist group. Since the Moros are Moslems, they have received support from Qaddafi, resulting in ex-President Marcos putting out a contract on the Libyan leader.

NAPAP. Ultra-left French terrorist group.

NAR (Nuclei Armati Revoluzionari). Right-wing Italian group responsible for the bombing of the Bologna Railway Station in 1980 and for assassinations and other acts.

NAYLP (National Arab Youth for the Liberation of Palestine). Formed by Colonel Qaddafi in 1972 and responsible for such acts as the thermite bombing of a Pan Am plane which resulted in the deaths of 32 persons and injuries to 18 others and a machine-gun attack on the passengers of a TWA flight in

Athens. Abu Nidal, who was involved in planning the *Achille Lauro* hijacking, was a prominent leader in the NAYLP, which seems to no longer exist.

Omega 7. U.S.-based, anti-Castro Cuban group, very active in New York City area, which carries out bombings of Cuban or pro-Cuban offices.

Onkruit. Dutch anti-NATO terrorist group.

OAS (Organisation de l'Armee Secrete). Anti-De Gaulle, expatriate French/Algerian terrorist group active in the 1960s which committed numerous bombings and attempted numerous assassinations of De Gaulle.

PFLP (Popular Front for the Liberation of Palestine). Palestinian terrorist group formed after the 1967 War and supported by Libya and other militant and/ or Communist states. The PFLP, under George Habish, established many ties with Western terrorist groups.

PIRA (Provisional Irish Republican Army). The "Provos" are a breakaway, militant, Marxist faction of the IRA which has carried out numerous terrorist acts in Northern Ireland and England.

RAF (Red Army Faction). The more "official" name for the Baader-Meinhof Gang of West German terrorists. The RAF has proven more resilient than many terrorist groups having resurgences despite large numbers of the members being imprisoned or killed. The kidnapping of Hans-Martin Schleyer and the hijacking of a Lufthansa plane to Mogadishu are among the RAF's best known operations.

Red Brigades. Italian left-wing terrorist group which emerged in the early 1970s. Many early members were disillusioned radical students. The Red Brigades did a great deal to destabilize Italy during the late Seventies, including the kidnapping and murder of Aldo Moro. Arson, assassination, bombing, and kidnapping have all been within the Red Brigades' venue. The Red Brigades have had close contact with the West German RAF and with the Italian Prima Linea and Azione Revoluzionaria groups.

Republik Malaku Selatan. South Moluccan separatist terrorist group which has carried out bombings and hijackings in Holland.

SDS (Students for a Democratic Society). Radical U.S. terrorist group active in the late 1960s and early Seventies as part of the anti-Vietnam War movement. The SDS carried out a great many bombings.

Sendero Luminuso (Shining Path). Peruvian terrorist/ Marxist guerrilla group which has carried out a large number of atrocities against Peruvian peasants.

SLA (Symbionese Liberation Army). U.S. terrorist group best known for kidnapping Patty Hearst.

TPLA (Turkish People's Liberation Army). Marxist Turkish terrorist confederation which has carried out hijackings, bombings, and assassinations. The TPLA has strong ties with the Palestinians and with Communist governments, the latter of which are very glad to encourage any group which will destabilize NATO member Turkey. The TPLA is most active within Turkey but has carried out external operations.

Tupamaros. Also known as MLN or *Movimiento de Liberation National.* Uruguayan terrorist/revolutionary group which was active in the 1960s but which is now virtually wiped out.

UDA (Ulster Defense Association). Protestant group formed to counter the IRA and keep Northern Ireland Protestant. Has engaged in murders and bombings among other terrorist acts. The Ulster Volunteer Force and Ulster Freedom Fighters are even more militant subgroups of the UDA.

Weather Underground. Primarily an anti-Vietnam War group, but some members were still involved in terrorist activities into the 1980s. The group has had links with the FALN and black militant groups.

Index

TYPICAL ORGANIZATION OF A HOSTAGE RESCUE UNIT

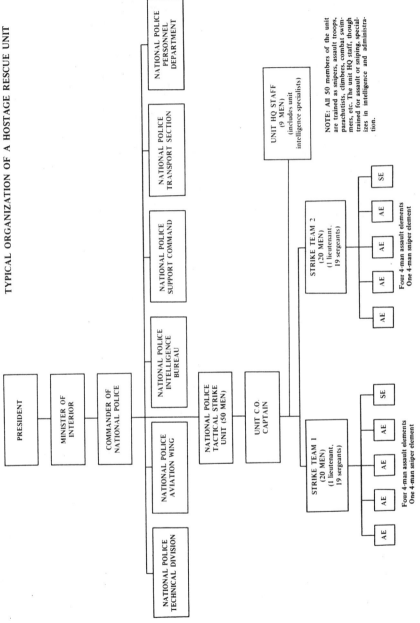

PRESIDENT

MINISTER OF INTERIOR

COMMANDER OF NATIONAL POLICE

NATIONAL POLICE TECHNICAL DIVISION

NATIONAL POLICE AVIATION WING

NATIONAL POLICE INTELLIGENCE BUREAU

NATIONAL POLICE SUPPORT COMMAND

NATIONAL POLICE TRANSPORT SECTION

NATIONAL POLICE PERSONNEL DEPARTMENT

NATIONAL POLICE TACTICAL STRIKE UNIT (50 MEN)

UNIT C.O. CAPTAIN

UNIT HQ STAFF (9 MEN) (includes unit intelligence specialists)

STRIKE TEAM 1 (20 MEN) (1 lieutenant, 19 sergeants)

AE AE AE AE SE

Four 4-man assault elements
One 4-man sniper element

STRIKE TEAM 2 (20 MEN) (1 lieutenant, 19 sergeants)

AE AE AE AE SE

Four 4-man assault elements
One 4-man sniper element

NOTE: All 50 members of the unit are trained as snipers, assault troops, parachutists, climbers, combat swimmers, etc. The unit HQ staff, though trained for assault or sniping, specializes in intelligence and administration.